vintage crochet
FOR YOUR home

Best-Loved Patterns for Afghans, Rugs and More from 1920—1959

Coats & Clark

kp
KRAUSE PUBLICATIONS
CINCINNATI, OHIO

Vintage Crochet for Your Home. Copyright © 2010 by Coats & Clark. Manufactured in China. All rights reserved. No part of this book may be reproduced in any form or by any electronic or mechanical means including information storage and retrieval systems without permission in writing from the publisher, except by a reviewer who may quote brief passages in a review. Published by Krause Publications, a division of F+W Media, Inc., 4700 East Galbraith Road, Cincinnati, Ohio, 45236. (800) 289-0963. First Edition.

14 13 12 11 10   5 4 3 2 1

DISTRIBUTED IN CANADA BY FRASER DIRECT
100 Armstrong Avenue
Georgetown, ON, Canada L7G 5S4
Tel: (905) 877-4411

DISTRIBUTED IN THE U.K. AND EUROPE BY DAVID & CHARLES
Brunel House, Newton Abbot, Devon, TQ12 4PU, England
Tel: (+44) 1626 323200, Fax: (+44) 1626 323319
Email: postmaster@davidandcharles.co.uk

DISTRIBUTED IN AUSTRALIA BY CAPRICORN LINK
P.O. Box 704, S. Windsor NSW, 2756 Australia
Tel: (02) 4577-3555

Library of Congress Cataloging in Publication Data
Vintage crochet for your home : best-loved patterns for afghans, rugs, and more / Coats & Clark.
     p. cm.
 Includes index.
 ISBN 978-1-4402-1370-0 (pbk. : alk. paper)
1. Crocheting--Patterns. 2. House furnishings. I. Coats & Clark.
 TT825.V55 2010
 746.43'4--dc22
                          2010017568

Edited by Christine Doyle

Designed by Dawn DeVries Sokol, Geoff Raker and Ronson Slagle

Production coordinated by Greg Nock

Photography by Al Parrish

Styling by Jan Nickum

www.fwmedia.com

Metric Conversion Chart

To convert	to	multiply by
Inches	Centimeters	2.54
Centimeters	Inches	0.4
Feet	Centimeters	30.5
Centimeters	Feet	0.03
Yards	Meters	0.9
Meters	Yards	1.1

Acknowledgments

We are unable to give the original designers their much deserved credit as the projects in this book originated in the 1920s to 1950s. Although the records of the original books don't exist, we believe the designers were all part of an in-house Coats & Clark design team. Their exquisite designs are even more incredible since they were more limited than we are in the colors and types of yarns and threads.

We'd like to acknowledge the special designers who have re-designed our vintage projects. Their names are featured with each project pattern herein. Our technical editor, Amy Polcyn, has made sure that the new patterns are written in a completely understandable style for today's crocheter. Our illustrator, Karen Manthey, has provided diagrams that are clear and precise. We appreciate their special talents.

Today our in-house design team continues to bring the best of yesterday's and today's needlecrafts along with the most contemporary product ideas to yarn users. We loved pouring over our archives to bring *Vintage Crochet for Your Home* to life and appreciate our wise, knowledgeable partners at Krause Publications.

Coats & Clark Design Team USA:

Nancy J. Thomas, *Creative Director*

Bobbie Matela, *Design Production Manager*

Catherine Babbie & Terri Geck, *Design Production Assistants*

Amy Olson, *Senior Product Manager Yarns*

Joan Barnett, *Product Manager Implements & Crochet Thread*

Kelly Schell, *Associate Product Manager*

Kathleen Sams, *Red Heart Ambassador*

Ann Blalock, *Manager Consumer Information*

Contents

Get Hooked on Vintage!

As a crocheter you have a distinct advantage in creating a home with warmth, originality and extra personality. As you look through the projects in this book, you will find ideas that crocheters from the 1920s to 1950s created using old brands such as Chadwick's and Clark's O.N.T. We've resurrected these designs from the Coats & Clark archives and asked designers to update the written patterns in today's vernacular and in yarns and threads that are readily available.

You'll be able to give your home one-of-a-kind style with projects for every room in the house. We've included projects for the kitchen, dining and entertaining, bed and bath and, of course, a wonderful collection of throws and afghans.

Whether you enjoy outfitting your rooms in totally retro style or are just adding a beautiful accent from the past to traditional or modern décor, *Vintage Crochet for Your Home* is full of ideas. You'll find crocheted accessories that will give your home more character, and you'll love being surrounded by these original pieces.

If your crochet skills need a little freshening up or you are new to crochet, we've included fully illustrated Crochet Basics in the back of this book for easy reference.

BEGINNER
Perfect for new crocheters, these projects use basic stitches and minimal shaping.

EASY
These projects use basic stitches, repetitive stitch patterns, simple color changes, and simple shaping and finishing. It's easy!

INTERMEDIATE
These projects use a variety of techniques, such as basic lace patterns or mid-level shaping, and are great for learning new skills.

History of Coats & Clark

With a rich heritage beginning in the early 1800s, Coats history is interwoven with many key innovations and historic events dating back to the beginnings of the industrial revolution. With nearly 200 years of history to share, we have selected a few interesting facts and images from our archives that we thought you would enjoy.

1812 — The Clarks opened the first factory for making cotton sewing thread in Paisley, Scotland. A few years later, another cotton thread mill was opened by James Coats.

1830 — The sons, James and Peter Coats, purchased their father's mill and, within a decade, J&P Coats Limited had expanded, with much of its production exported to America. Another member of the family, Andrew Coats, was sent to the U.S. to manage the business.

1864 — George and William Clark, grandsons of James Clark, opened a cotton thread mill in Newark, New Jersey. Five years later, the Coats family began manufacturing thread in Pawtucket, Rhode Island, selling under the name The Spool Cotton Company.

1896 — The company continued to grow by adding new products and innovations, including crochet, darning, knitting and embroidery cottons. O.N.T. ("Our New Thread") was the first genuinely fast black thread and the first American brand of sewing, crochet and embroidery cotton to be offered in a large range of colors, all colorfast to boiling.

1952 — J&P Coats and the Clark Thread Co. merged to become Coats & Clark Inc.

1960s — Coats & Clark created cotton-covered polyester core thread, which combined the best characteristics of both fibers and made it compatible with new fibers and fabrics that had entered the market. Today, Coats Dual Duty Plus® is the number-one selling all-purpose thread in the home sewing market.

Coats worldwide continues to innovate. Through ongoing research and product development, new fibers, fabrics, finishes and their application for consumer and industrial applications are explored.

CLARK'S O.N.T. SPOOL COTTON. "TESTING"

About Red Heart

In 1935, J&P Coats USA saw a need in the market for wool yarn and set the stage for the development and growth of one of today's most recognized and best known brands in the marketplace, Red Heart.

At that time, Patons & Baldwins UK was known for its world famous and affluent Beehive wool yarns and

the company needed a distribution agent in the U.S. Coats agreed to market the imported Patons & Baldwins Beehive yarns in the U.S. and to manufacture a new lower-priced wool yarn through its subsidiary The Spool Cotton Company.

The new yarn was called Red Heart and was represented with a heart symbol, a trademarked icon previously used by Patons & Baldwins. The first wool yarn processing plant was built in Newark, New Jersey. The finished yarns, which were branded Chadwick's Red Heart, went to market in September, 1936.

Other notable dates in the history of Red Heart include:

1947—The Spool Cotton Company began nationally advertising Chadwick's Red Heart yarns in women's magazines.

1947—Manufacturing operations moved from Newark, New Jersey to Albany, Georgia, where they remain today.

1952—Red Heart introduced the Tangle-Proof center-pull skein.

HARD TO BEAT.

1955—The brand name changed from Chadwick Red Heart to Coats & Clark Red Heart.

1959—Coats & Clark introduced Red Heart Orlon acrylic yarn—Orlon was the name of a new synthetic fiber from DuPont.

1967—Introduced Red Heart Wintuk yarns

1980s—Susan Bates became a division of Coats & Clark with crochet and knitting tools and accessories

1987—Introduced Red Heart Super Saver® (article E300), featuring no-dye-lot solids and superior wash performance

1991—Aunt Lydia's brand of crochet threads acquired from American Thread

1988—Changed name of Red Heart 4 Ply Handknitting Yarn to Red Heart Classic

1998—Launched TLC brand with TLC ultra-soft yarn (article E510)

2004—Launched Moda Dea brand with seven fashion yarns

2008—Introduced two new Red Heart eco-yarns using recycled fibers—Red Heart Eco-Cotton Blend and Red Heart Eco-Ways

2010—Introduced a new line of natural fiber yarns—Stitch Nation by Debbie Stoller

Today, Red Heart is an internationally renowned brand offering more than 20 different yarns under its label in the U.S. alone.

SMALL THINGS OF GREAT IMPORTANCE

Here is your chance to introduce a gay note of individuality into your kitchen. Whether it's pure color—crisp modern— or provincial in flavor—these pot holders will serve a decorative as well as a useful purpose.

DIRECTIONS ON PAGES 20 AND 21

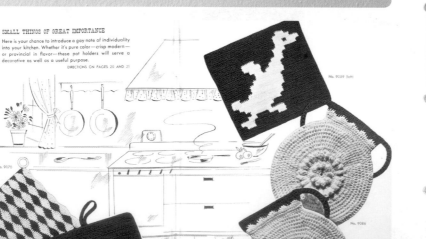

No. 9059 (left)

No. 9070

No. 9086

"Mosaic" Pot Holder A-502

J. & P. COATS "KNIT-CRO-SHEEN": 1 ball of No. 150 Blended Pink & Hunter. Milwards Steel Crochet Hook No. 7.

1 bone ring; a piece of felt for lining.

MOTIF . . . Starting at center, ch 2. 1st rnd: 6 sc in 2nd ch from hook. Join with sl st in first sc. 2nd rnd: Ch 1, 2 sc in joining, 2 sc in each sc around. Join to first sc— 12 sc. 3rd rnd: Ch 1, 2 sc in joining, sc in next sc, * 2 sc in next sc, sc in next sc. Repeat from * around. Join—18 sc. 4th rnd: * Insert hook in next sc, thread over and draw loop through to

measure ½ inch, thread over and draw through 2 loops on hook—long sc made; ch 1. Repeat from * 11 times more. Join to first long sc. 5th rnd: Ch 1, sc in joining, sc in next ch, * sc in next long sc, sc in next ch. Repeat from * around. Join— 24 sc. 6th rnd: Ch 1, 2 sc in joining, sc in next 2 sc, * 2 sc in next sc, sc in next 2 sc. Repeat from * around. Join—32 sc. 7th rnd: Ch 1, sc in joining, * sc in next sc, make 3 dc, dc and h dc dfor corner), sc in next 7 sc. Repeat from * around, ending with sc in last 6 sc. Join. Break off and fasten.

Make 19 more motifs. Sew 4 x 5 motifs neatly together. Press lightly; line with felt.

Ring: Sc closely around ring. Sew to any corner.

[17]

Chapter One

Kitchen Aids

Add some vintage-inspired charm to your kitchen. You'll find colorful florals and interesting mitered dishcloths that are perfect for kitchen clean ups. Pot holders are fashioned in a graphic hopscotch pattern or in the shape of a retro pitcher. Old patterns for crocheted shopping bags are revived as thrifty and ecological choices for today.

Garden of Dishcloths

The original Coats & Clark booklet encouraged the homemaker of the mid-1900s to choose her favorite flower pot holder—sunflower, pansy or dahlia—to brighten her kitchen. We think these are a bit too holey to use for taking something out of the oven. So we suggest using them as dishcloths to brighten your mood at the kitchen sink. Or hang them on the wall or refrigerator to add a colorful kitchen accent.

Adapted by Mary Ann Frits

Dahlia

SIZES: *One size*

FINISHED MEASUREMENTS:
   Approx 6" × 10" (15cm × 25cm), excluding leaves

YARN:

1 skein Coats Crème de la Crème® Solids (combed cotton, 126 yds [115m] per 71g skein) in each of colors #0905 Rally Red (A), #0649 Forest (C)

1 skein Coats Crème de la Crème® Multis (combed cotton, 99 yds [90m] per 57g skein) in color #0992 Bowl of Cherries (B)

HOOK: *Size H (5mm) crochet hook*

NOTIONS: *Yarn needle*

GAUGE: *14 sts = 4" (10cm) in pattern*

Pansy

SIZES: *One size*

FINISHED MEASUREMENTS:
   Approx 7½" × 9½" (19cm × 24cm)

YARN:

1 skein Coats Crème de la Crème® Solids (combed cotton, 126 yds [115m] per 71g skein) in each of colors #0205 Golden Yellow (A), #0910 Wood Violet (B), #0679 Spruce (D)

1 skein Coats Crème de la Crème® Multis (combed cotton, 99 yds [90m] per 57g skein) in color #0993 Snow Violet Ombre (C)

HOOK: *Size H (5mm) crochet hook*

NOTIONS: *Yarn needle*

GAUGE: *17 sts = 4" (10cm) in pattern*

Sunflower

SIZES: *One size*

FINISHED MEASUREMENTS:
   Approx 6½" × 10¼" (17cm × 26cm), excluding leaves

YARN:

1 skein Coats Crème de la Crème® Solids (combed cotton, 126 yds [115m] per 71g skein) in each of colors #0331 Fudge Brown (A), #0501 Aqua Jade (C)

1 skein Coats Crème de la Crème® Multis (combed cotton, 99 yds [90m] per 57g skein) in color #0960 Goldtones (B)

HOOK: *Size H (5mm) crochet hook*

NOTIONS: *Yarn needle*

GAUGE: *17 sts = 4" (10cm) in pattern*

Garden of Dishcloths

Dahlia

Center

With A, ch 4, join with slip st to form a ring.

Round 1 (RS): Ch 1, 6 sc in ring. Do not join.

Round 2: Ch 1, [sc, ch 5] twice in each sc around. Do not join.

Round 3: Sc in first sc, ch 1, holding loops forward, *sc in next sc, ch 1; repeat from * around, join with slip st in first sc. Fasten off.

Petals

Round 1 (RS): Join B with sc in any ch-1 space, *(hdc, 3 dc, hdc) in next ch-1 space **, sc in next ch-1 space; repeat from * around, ending last repeat at **; join with slip st in first sc.

Round 2: Ch 1, sc in back of same sc as joining, holding petals forward, *ch 3, sc in base of center dc on next petal, ch 3 **, sc in back of next sc; repeat from * around, ending last repeat at **. Do not join.

Round 3: (Sc, hdc, dc, tr, dc, hdc, sc) in each ch-3 space around, join in first sc.

Round 4: Ch 2, holding petals forward, *sc in base of next tr on next petal, ch 5; repeat from * around, join in first sc.

Round 5: (Sc, hdc, dc, 3 tr, dc, hdc, sc) in each ch-5 space around, join in first sc. Fasten off.

Stem

With C, ch 16; hdc in 3rd ch from hook, hdc in next ch, *2 hdc in next ch, hdc in each of next 3 ch; repeat from * across. Fasten off.

Leaf

Make 2.

With C, ch 15.

Row 1 (RS): Sc in 2nd ch from hook, hdc in next ch, dc in next ch, 2 tr in each of next 2 ch, tr in each of next 3 ch, 2 dc in next ch, dc in each of next 2 ch, hdc in next ch, sc in next ch, 3 sc in last ch; working in unused loops on opposite side of beginning ch, hdc in each of next 3 ch, 2 dc in each of next 2 ch, 2 tr in next ch, tr in each of next 4 ch, dc in next ch, hdc in next ch, sc in each of next 2 ch, join with slip st in first sc.

Round 2: Slip st in each st around, join in joining slip st. Fasten off.

Finishing

Sew one leaf to each side of stem. Sew stem to flower.

Weave in ends.

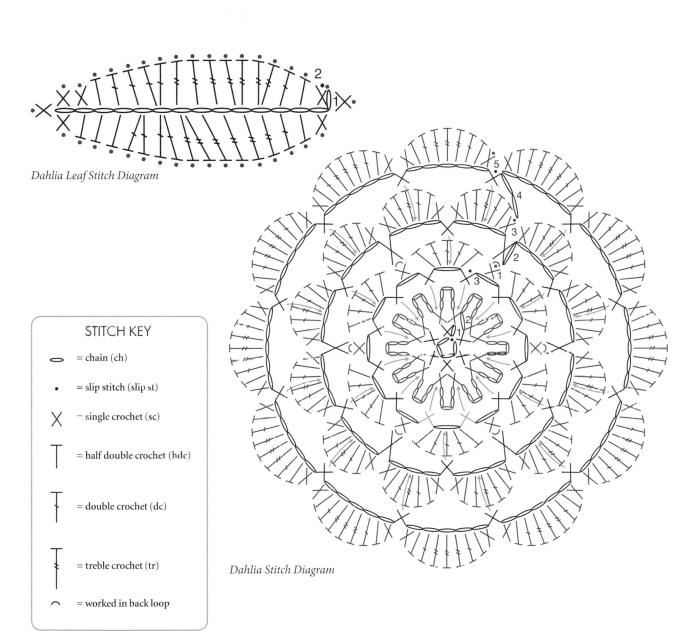

Dahlia Leaf Stitch Diagram

STITCH KEY

⬯ = chain (ch)

• = slip stitch (slip st)

✕ = single crochet (sc)

T = half double crochet (hdc)

Ŧ = double crochet (dc)

Ŧ = treble crochet (tr)

⌒ = worked in back loop

Dahlia Stitch Diagram

Dahlia Stem Stitch Diagram

Garden of Dishcloths

Pansy

First 3 Petals

With A, ch 5, join with slip st to form a ring.

Round 1 (RS): Ch 1, 12 sc in ring. Do not join.

Round 2: *(Sc, hdc, dc) in next sc, 2 tr in each of next 2 sc, (dc, hdc, sc) in next sc; repeat from * twice; change to B by drawing loop through; join with sc in first sc. Fasten off A.

Round 3: *Hdc in next hdc, 2 dc in next dc, 2 tr in each of next 4 tr, 2 dc in next dc, hdc in next hdc, sc in next sc, skip next sc; repeat from * once; hdc in next hdc, 2 dc in next dc, 2 tr in each of next 4 tr, 2 dc in next dc, hdc in next hdc. Do not join.

Round 4: *Sc in next sc, (hdc, dc) in next st, 2 tr in each of next 12 sts, (dc, hdc) in next st, sc in next sc; repeat from * around, skip first sc, join with sc in front loop of first hdc.

Round 5: Working in front loops only, sc in each st around; join with slip st in first sc.

Fourth Petal

Row 1: Ch 1, working in back loops of Round 4, skip first st, sc in next st, * ch 3, skip next 3 sts, sc in next st; repeat from * 3 times more. Fasten off.

Row 2: Join C in first sc, ch 5, [dtr, ch 3, slip st in top of dtr just made] 6 times in each of next 3 ch-3 spaces; skip next space, slip st in last sc. Fasten off.

Fifth Petal

Row 1: Skip first 10 back loops on Round 4 of third petal, working in back loops on Round 4, join B with sc in next st, [ch 3, skip next 3 sts, sc in next st] 3 times. Fasten off.

Row 2: Join C with slip st in first sc, (hdc, ch 3, slip st in top of hdc just made, [dc, ch 3, slip st in top of dc just made] twice, [tr, ch 3, slip st in top of tr just made] twice) in first ch-3 space, [dtr, ch 3, slip st in

top of dtr just made] 8 times in each of next 2 ch-3 spaces, holding the first 6 dtr of 4th petal forward, join with slip st in back of next dtr on 4th petal. Fasten off.

Leaf

Make 2.

With D, ch 13.

Row 1 (RS): Sc in 2nd ch from hook, 2 hdc in next ch, 2 dc in next ch, 2 tr in next ch, dtr in each of next 4 ch, 2 dtr in each of next 3 ch, 7 tr in last ch; working in unused loops on opposite side of beginning ch, 2 tr in each of next 2 ch, dtr in each of next 5 ch, tr in next ch, dc in next ch, hdc in next ch, sc in next ch, join with slip st in first sc.

Round 2: Slip st in each st around, join with slip st in joining slip st. Fasten off.

Finishing

Sew leaves to flower as shown. Weave in ends.

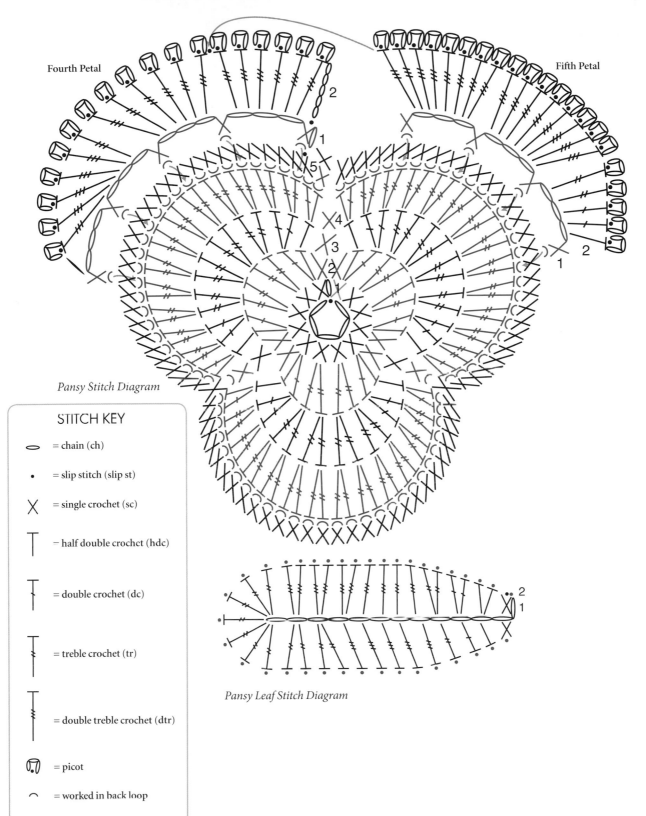

Fourth Petal

Fifth Petal

Pansy Stitch Diagram

Pansy Leaf Stitch Diagram

STITCH KEY

◯ = chain (ch)

• = slip stitch (slip st)

✕ = single crochet (sc)

T = half double crochet (hdc)

T = double crochet (dc)

T = treble crochet (tr)

T = double treble crochet (dtr)

⬭ = picot

⌢ = worked in back loop

⌣ = worked in front loop

Garden of Dishcloths

Sunflower

Center

With A, ch 5, join with slip st to form a ring.

Round 1 (RS): Ch 1, 11 sc in ring. Do not join.

Round 2: Ch 1, *4 sc in next sc, drop loop from hook, insert hook from front to back in first sc made, draw dropped loop through, ch 1 tightly (pc made); repeat from * around, join with slip st in first pc. Fasten off.

Petals

Round 1 (RS): Join B with sc in any ch-1 space, *ch 9, slip st in 2nd ch from hook, slip st in each remaining ch, ch 1, skip next pc, sc in next ch-1 space; repeat from * 9 times more, ch 9, slip st in 2nd ch from hook, slip st in each remaining ch, ch 1, join with slip st in first sc.

Round 2: *Working in unused loops of next ch-9, skip next ch, dc in each of next 4 ch, hdc in next ch, sc in next 2 ch, 3 sc in next ch; working in unused top loops of same ch as slip sts made on Round 1, sc in next 2 ch, hdc in next ch, dc in each of next 4 ch, skip next ch **, slip st in next sc; repeat from * around, ending last repeat at **, join with slip st in joining slip st.

Round 3: Ch 1, working behind petals, *sc in back of first sc on Round 1, ch 9, slip st in 2nd ch from hook, slip st in each remaining ch, ch 1; repeat from * around; join with slip st in back of next sc on Round 1.

Round 4: *Working in unused loops of next ch-9, skip next ch, dc in each of next 4 ch, hdc in next ch, sc in next 2 ch, 3 sc in next ch; working in unused top loops of same ch as slip sts made on Round 3, sc in next 2 ch, hdc in next ch, dc in each of next 4 ch, skip next ch, slip st in next sc; repeat from * around. Fasten off.

Stem

With C, ch 2.

Row 1 (RS): 2 sc in 2nd ch from hook, ch 1, turn.

Row 2: 2 sc in first sc, sc in next sc, ch 1, turn.

Row 3: Sc in each sc, ch 1, turn.

Rows 4-9: Repeat Row 3. Fasten off.

Leaf

Make 2.

With C, ch 15.

Row 1 (RS): Sc in 2nd ch from hook, hdc in next ch, dc in next ch, 2 tr in next ch, tr in each of next 4 ch, 2 dc in next ch, dc in each of next 2 ch, hdc in next ch, sc in next ch, 3 sc in last ch; working in unused loops on opposite side of beginning ch, hdc in each of next 3 ch, 2 dc in next ch, 2 tr in next ch, tr in each of next 5 ch, dc in next ch, hdc in next ch, sc in next ch, join with slip st in first sc.

Round 2: Slip st in each st around, join in joining slip st. Fasten off.

Finishing

Sew one leaf to each side of stem. Sew stem to flower. Weave in ends.

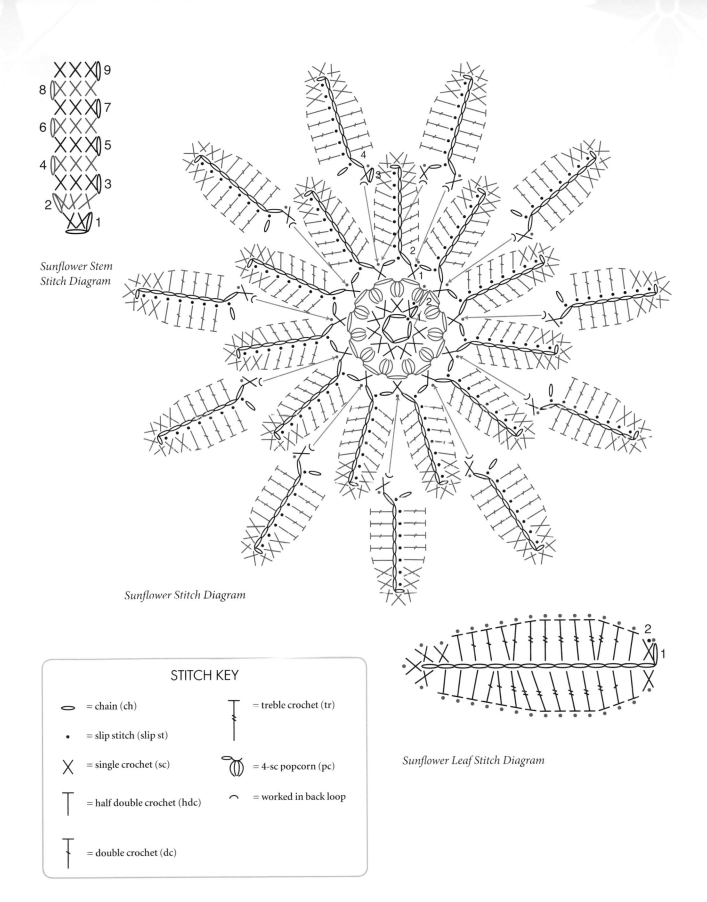

*Sunflower Stem
Stitch Diagram*

Sunflower Stitch Diagram

Sunflower Leaf Stitch Diagram

STITCH KEY

⬭ = chain (ch)

• = slip stitch (slip st)

✕ = single crochet (sc)

T = half double crochet (hdc)

╪ = double crochet (dc)

╫ = treble crochet (tr)

🮲 = 4-sc popcorn (pc)

⌣ = worked in back loop

Hopscotch Pot Holders

We're not sure why last century's designer thought these looked like a hopscotch, but we love the light-hearted graphic feel of this design. Surface chain stitch embroidery brings out the curvy lines. These are made double, so they work as pot holders.

Adapted by
Nancy Anderson

SIZES: *One size*

FINISHED MEASUREMENTS: *8"*
(20cm) square, after blocking

THREAD:

Teal Version

1 ball Aunt Lydia's® Fashion Crochet Thread Size 3 (mercerized cotton, 150 yds [137m] per 2.21 oz ball) in color #65 Warm Teal (A)

2 balls Aunt Lydia's® Fashion Crochet Thread Size 3 (mercerized cotton, 150 yds [137m] per 2.21 oz ball) in each of colors #365 Coffee (B) and #926 Bridal White (C)

Rose Version

1 ball Aunt Lydia's® Fashion Crochet Thread Size 3 (mercerized cotton, 150 yds [137m] per 2.21 oz ball) in color #775 Warm Rose (A)

2 balls Aunt Lydia's® Fashion Crochet Thread Size 3 (mercerized cotton, 150 yds [137m] per 2.21 oz ball) in each of colors #926 Bridal White (B) and #365 Coffee (C)

HOOK: *Size E (3.5mm) crochet hook*

NOTIONS:

Yarn needle

Sharp embroidery needle

¾" (2cm) plastic ring

GAUGE: *1 motif = 3¼" (8cm) square*
20 dc and 12 rows = 4" (10cm)

Hopscotch Pot Holders

NOTE: *Each double-layered pot holder consists of 4 motifs stitched together for the front and a back piece worked in dc.*

Pot Holder

Motif

Make 4.

Round 1: With A, ch 4, dc 23 sts in 4th ch from hook, join with slip st in top of ch-4.

Round 2: Ch 5, dtr in same st, ch 5 and join with slip st in same st, * sc in next dc, skip next dc, 5 dc in next dc, skip next dc, sc in next dc, slip st in next dc, ch 5, dtr, ch 5 and join with slip st in same st; repeat from * twice more, sc in next dc, skip next dc, 5 dc in next dc, skip next dc, sc in next dc. Join to first ch of ch-5. Fasten off.

Round 3: Join B to any dtr, ch 1, sc in same space, * (tr, 4 dc) in next sc, skip next 2 dc, sc in back loop of next dc, skip next 2 dc, (4 dc, tr) in next sc, sc in next dtr; repeat from * around. Join last tr to first sc. Drop B.

Round 4: Join C to back loop of join, draw thread through loop on hook and, working over thread to conceal it, ch 3, work 4 dc in join, yo, insert hook in same joining, yo and draw through loop, yo and draw through 2 loops on hook, drop C and pick up B, yo and draw B through 2 loops on hook (color change made—always change colors in this manner), * working over unused color, skip next tr and dc in next 9 sts, changing color on next to last dc, skip next tr, 5 dc in corner sc, changing color on last dc; repeat from * around, changing color on 9th dc, join to top of ch-3.

Round 5: With B, ch 3, dc in next dc, * 5 dc in center dc of corner, dc in next 2 dc, changing color on last dc, skip dc, dc in next 7 sts, changing color on last dc, dc in last "B" dc and in next dc; repeat from * around, ending with a "C" dc in last dc. Join with slip st to top of ch-3.

Round 6: Ch 3, dc in next 3 dc, *5 dc in center dc of corner, dc in next 4 dc, changing color on last dc, skip dc & dc in in next 5 sts, changing color on last dc, dc in next 6 dc. Repeat from * around, ending in 2 B dc. Join & finish off both colors.

Back

Make 1.

With B, ch 39.

Row 1: Dc in 4th ch from hook and each ch across—36 dc.

Rows 2-21: Ch 3, dc across.

Next Round: Ch 1, work sc evenly around, working 3 sc in each corner. Join with slip st.

Next Round: Join A, ch 2, * hdc in each st across to corner st, hdc 3 times in corner st; repeat from * around and join with slip st to beginning ch-2.

Finishing

Sew motifs together, matching colors carefully (change thread color to match the motif color for invisible seams). Weave in ends.

Next Round: With A, ch 1, and sc around Front, working 3 sc in each corner. Join with slip st. Do not fasten off.

With A and embroidery needle, outline the circular patterns using an embroidery chain stitch as shown below.

Pin front to back with wrong sides together. With A, ch 1 and sc around, making certain to include both layers. Weave in ends. Block to size.

Hanging Loop

Join A to plastic ring, ch 1 and sc tightly around. Fasten off. Sew in place to corner of pot holder. Weave in ends.

Embroidery Stitch Illustration

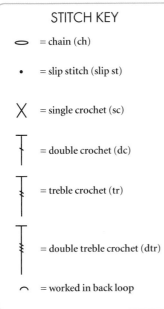

STITCH KEY	
⬯	= chain (ch)
•	= slip stitch (slip st)
✕	= single crochet (sc)
⊤	= double crochet (dc)
⨍	= treble crochet (tr)
	= double treble crochet (dtr)
⌒	= worked in back loop

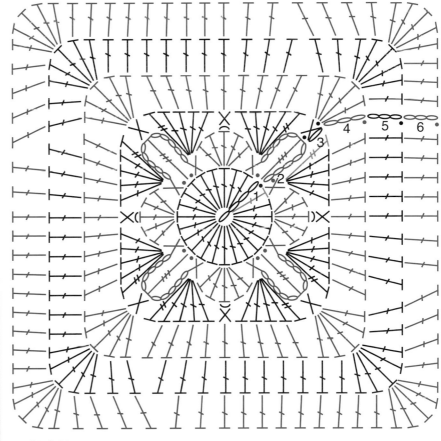

Stitch Diagram

Mitered Dishcloths

EASY

These dishcloths may have been conceived in the 1940s, but this mitered technique is contemporary. When choosing your yarn, keep in mind that the multi-colored stripes will stand out more clearly if the solid color background does not appear within the multi-color yarn. We love the way the ridges help rub dried food off the dishes.

*Adapted by
Andee Graves*

SIZES: *One size*

FINISHED MEASUREMENTS:
  7" (18cm) square

YARN:

Green Version

1 skein Coats Crème de la Crème® Solids (combed cotton, 126 yds [115m] per 71g skein) in color #625 Brite Green (A)

1 skein Coats Crème de la Crème® Multis (combed cotton, 99 yds [90m] per 57g skein) in color #993 Snow Violet Ombre (B)

Violet Version

1 skein Coats Crème de la Crème® Solids (combed cotton, 126 yds [115m] per 71g skein) in color #910 Wood Violet (A)

1 skein Coats Crème de la Crème® Multis (combed cotton, 99 yds [90m] per 57g skein) in color #941 Caribbean Cool (B)

HOOK: *Size H (5mm) crochet hook*

NOTIONS: *Yarn needle*

GAUGE: *19 dc and 11 rows = 4" (10cm)*

STITCH KEY

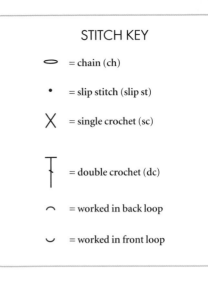

◯ = chain (ch)

• = slip stitch (slip st)

✕ = single crochet (sc)

┬ = double crochet (dc)

⌒ = worked in back loop

⌣ = worked in front loop

Note: Green sts are worked in rem loops on RS of dishcloth. Red sts are worked in rem loops on WS of dishcloth.

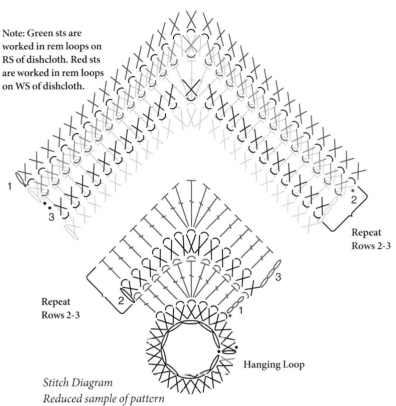

Repeat
Rows 2-3

Repeat
Rows 2-3

Hanging Loop

Stitch Diagram
Reduced sample of pattern

Dishcloth

Hanging Loop

With B, ch 10 and join with a slip st to form a ring. Ch 1 and work 25 sc in ring. Fasten off, leaving a 6-8" (15-20cm) tail.

Note: Work all sts in the back loop only through Row 20.

Row 1 (RS): With RS of hanging loop facing, join A in a sc and pull up a loop. Ch 3, dc in next 2 sc, 5 dc in next sc, dc in next 3 sc. Ch 1, turn.

Row 2: Sc across, working 3 sc in 3rd st of 5-dc group. End with sc in 3rd ch of beginning ch-3, ch 3, turn.

Row 3: Dc across, working 5 dc in 2nd st of center 3-sc group, ch 1, turn.

Rows 4-20: Repeat Rows 2 and 3, ending with Row 2. Fasten off.

Contrast Striping

Note: Contrast Striping rows are worked back over the piece from last row of cloth to ring, working in the free loops of each row and turning cloth after each row to create stripes on front and back.

Row 1 (WS): With WS facing and hanging loop at bottom, join B in right corner of cloth and pull up a loop in first st. Ch 1, sc in free loop of each sc across. Loosely slip st into side of row and turn work.

Row 2: Working into free loops of dc on next row above, sc across row. Work 2 loose slip sts into side of row, turn work.

Row 3: Working into free loops of sc on next row above, sc across row. Work 1 loose slip st into side of row, turn work.

Rows 4-20: Repeat Rows 2 and 3, ending with Row 2.

Row 21: Work 7 surface chains evenly into spaces at base of loop where first row of dc is attached. Fasten off.

Finishing

Weave in ends.

Café-au-Lait Pot Holder

This clever pitcher was a popular shape used for coffee creamers. We suggest choosing a shade of crochet thread that coordinates with your dinnerware. Or maybe keep it handy next to a modern day espresso machine while frothing milk for your latté.

Adapted by
Sharon Mann

SIZES: *One size*

FINISHED MEASUREMENTS: *6½"*
  (17cm) diameter

THREAD:

2 balls Aunt Lydia's® Fashion Crochet
  Thread Size 3 (mercerized cotton,
  150 yds [137m] per 2.2 oz ball) in
  color #0930 Monet (A)

1 ball Aunt Lydia's® Fashion Crochet
  Thread Size 3 (mercerized cotton,
  150 yds [137m] per 2.2 oz ball) in
  color #0486 Navy (B)

HOOK: *Size 6 (1.8mm) steel crochet*
  hook

NOTIONS: *Yarn needle*

GAUGE: *7 sts = 1" (2.5cm) in pattern*

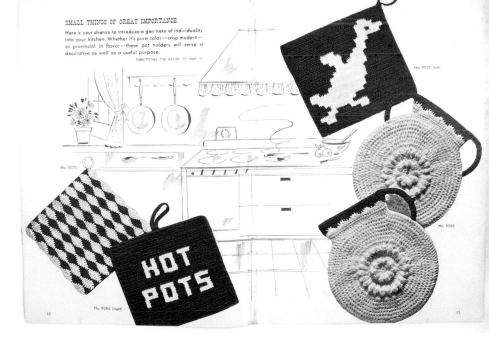

SPECIAL ABBREVIATION:

Tr-pc (triple popcorn): 5 tr in same st, drop loop from hook, insert hook through first tr and draw dropped loop through first tr, ch 1 tightly.

Café-au-Lait Pot Holder

Pot Holder

Make 2.

Round 1: With A, ch 2, 10 sc in 2nd ch from hook, join with slip st to first st.

Round 2: Ch 4 (counts as tr), 4 tr in first st, **drop loop from hook, insert hook through first tr and draw dropped loop through first tr **, ch 1 tightly (tr-pc made), *ch 2, 5 tr in next st, repeat ** to **; repeat from * 8 more times, ch 2, slip st to first ch 1 in first tr-pc—10 tr-pc clusters.

Round 3: Ch 3 (counts as dc), 2 dc in back of tr-pc, *2 dc in ch-2 space, 2 dc in back of next tr-pc; repeat from * around increasing 4 sts evenly, 2 dc in last ch-2 space—44 dc.

Round 4: Ch 4 (counts as tr), complete tr-pc, ch 2, skip next dc, *tr-pc, ch 2, skip next dc; repeat from * around, slip st to first ch 1 in first tr-pc—22 tr-pc clusters.

Round 5: Ch 3, *4 dc in next ch-2 space; repeat from * around, 3 dc in last ch-2 space, slip st to top of ch-3—88 dc.

Round 6: Ch 3 (counts as dc), dc in next 6 sts, 2 dc in next st, *dc in next 7 sts, 2 dc in next st; repeat from * around, slip st to top of ch-3—99 dc.

Round 7: Ch 3 (counts as dc), dc in next 7 sts, 2 dc in next st, *dc in next 8 sts, 2 dc in next st; repeat from * around, slip st to top of ch-3—110 dc.

Round 8: Ch 3 (counts as dc), dc in next 8 sts, 2 dc in next st, *dc in next 9 sts, 2 dc in next st; repeat from * around, slip st to top of ch-3—121 dc.

Now work in rows:

Row 1: Ch 3 (counts as dc), dc in same st, dc in next 2 sts, hdc in next 3 sts, sc in next 13 sts, hdc in next 3 sts, dc in next 2 sts, 2 dc in next st, turn—27 sts.

Row 2: Ch 1, 2 sc in first 2 sts, sc across, 2 sc in last 2 sts—31 sts.

Row 3: Ch 1, *sc, hdc, dc, tr, dc, hdc; repeat from * across, ending with sc, turn.

Row 4: Change to B, ch 4 in first st, *dc in hdc, hdc in dc, sc in tr, hdc in dc, dc in hdc, tr in sc; repeat from * across, turn.

Row 5: Ch 1, sc in first st, sc in each st across. Fasten off.

Handle

Make 1.

With B, ch 27.

Row 1: Sc in 2nd ch from hook, sc in each st across, turn—26 sts.

Row 2: Sc in first st, sc in each st across, turn.

Row 3: Repeat Row 2. Fasten off.

Weave in ends. Fold handle in half and sew side seam.

Finishing

Weave in ends on each pot holder. Pin cup handle in place at the top right-hand side of cup. WS facing, sew both sides together.

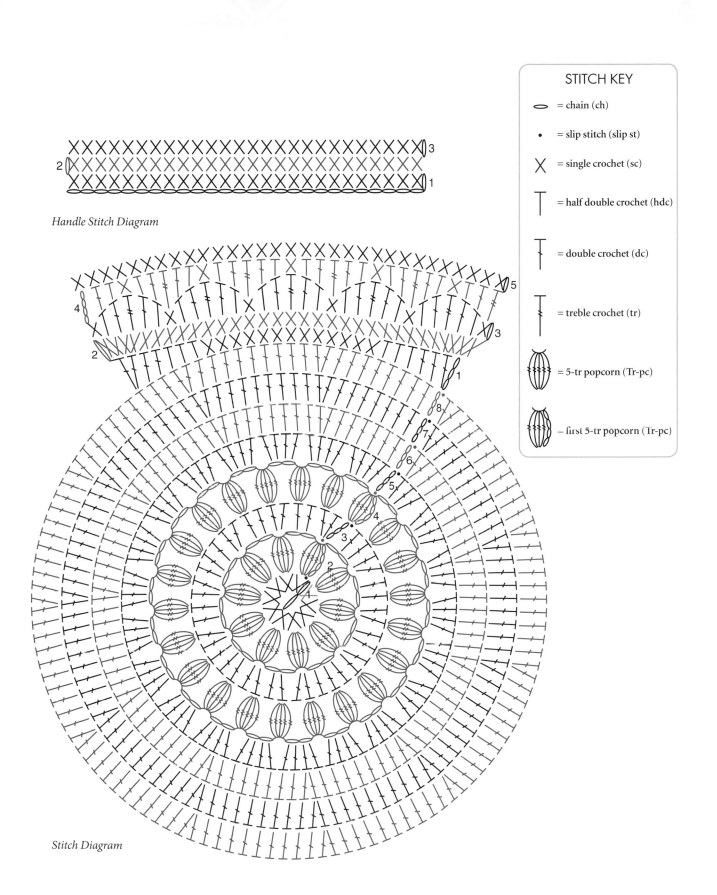

Handle Stitch Diagram

Stitch Diagram

STITCH KEY

⬭ = chain (ch)

• = slip stitch (slip st)

✕ = single crochet (sc)

┬ = half double crochet (hdc)

┬ = double crochet (dc)

┬ = treble crochet (tr)

= 5-tr popcorn (Tr-pc)

= first 5-tr popcorn (Tr-pc)

To Market, To Market Shopping Bag

Imagine the maker of this bag getting onto the streetcar with her daily purchases from the food market or bakery and emptying them into her icebox. Today this reusable bag is an ecological choice even though you may get into your own car and store your food in a roomy side-by-side refrigerator.

Adapted by Sharon Mann

SIZES: *One size*

FINISHED MEASUREMENTS: *18" × 13" (46cm × 33cm), excluding handles*

YARN:

2 skeins Red Heart® Eco-Cotton™ Blend (recycled cotton/acrylic, 145 yds [132m] per 3 oz skein) in color #1926 Currant

HOOK: *Size E (3.5mm) crochet hook*

NOTIONS: *Yarn needle*

GAUGE: *17 sts = 4" (10cm) in pattern*

SPECIAL ABBREVIATION:

Trtr (triple treble crochet):

Wrap yarn over hook 4 times, insert hook in base st, * pull yarn through 2 loops; repeat from * 4 more times, until there is 1 loop on hook.

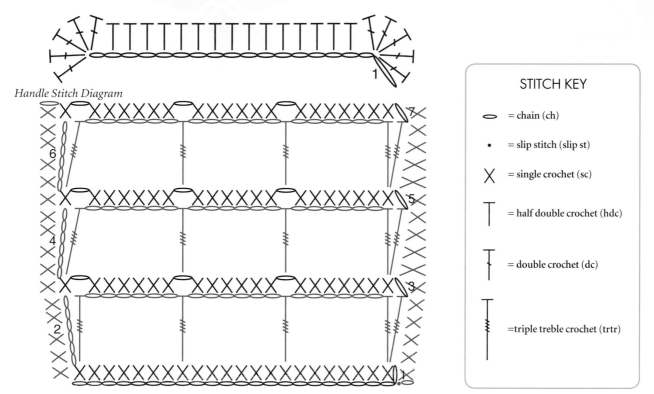

Handle Stitch Diagram

Bag Stitch Diagram

STITCH KEY

- ⬭ = chain (ch)
- • = slip stitch (slip st)
- ✕ = single crochet (sc)
- ⊤ = half double crochet (hdc)
- ⊤ = double crochet (dc)
- ⊤ =triple treble crochet (trtr)

Bag

Ch 79.

Row 1 (RS): Sc in 2nd ch from hook, sc in each ch across, turn —78 sc.

Row 2: Ch 6, wrap yarn over hook 4 times, insert hook in same st, * pull yarn through 2 loops; repeat from * 4 more times, until there is 1 loop on hook (trtr made); ** ch 6, wrap yarn around hook 4 times, skip 6 sts, insert hook in next st, *** pull yarn through 2 loops; repeat from *** 4 more times; repeat from ** across; make 2 trtr in last st, turn.

Row 3: Ch 1, sc in 2nd st from hook, * 6 sc in ch-6 space, ch 1; repeat from * across, sc in last st, turn.

Row 4: Ch 6, wrap yarn over hook 4 times, insert hook in same st, * pull yarn through 2 loops; repeat from * 4 more times, until there is 1 loop on hook (trtr made); ** ch 6, wrap yarn around hook 4 times, skip 6 sts, insert hook in next st, *** pull yarn through 2 loops; repeat from *** 4 more

times; repeat from ** across; make 2 trtr in last st, turn.

Repeat Rows 3 and 4 until piece measures 26" (66cm), ending with Row 3. Slip st across next row. Fasten off.

Handles

Make 2.

Ch 93.

Row 1: Dc in 2nd ch from hook, 4 dc in same st, hdc in each ch across to last ch, 5 dc in last ch. Fasten off.

Finishing

Sc evenly along each long side of bag as follows: * sc in first st, 4 sc in outside trtr, sc in sc row; repeat from * across. With RS facing, fold bag in half and sew side seams. Sew handles in place at top. Weave in ends.

Long Shopping Bag

EASY

The writer of this shopping bag pattern encouraged crocheters to make up this smart utility bag in "gay colors." We didn't take her advice when choosing our eco-minded cotton yarn in almond. But it does excite us to have such a handy reusable bag that will last for years!

*Adapted by
Sharon Mann*

SIZES: *One size*

FINISHED MEASUREMENTS: *18″ × 13″ (46cm × 33cm), excluding handles*

YARN:

2 skeins Red Heart® Eco-Cotton™ Blend (recycled cotton/acrylic, 145 yds [132m] per 3 oz skein) in color #1340 Almond

HOOK: *Size G (4.25mm) crochet hook*

NOTIONS: *Yarn needle*

GAUGE: *13 sts = 4″ (10cm) in pattern*

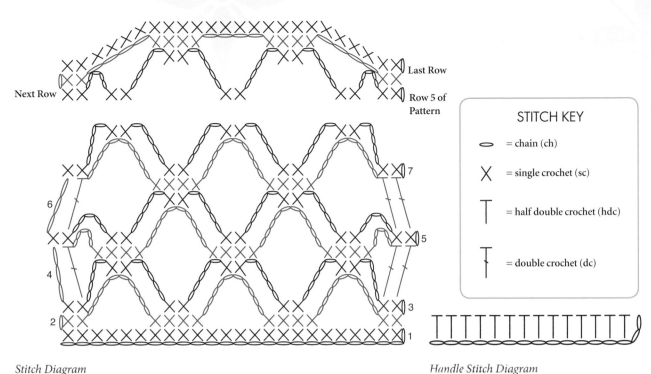

STITCH KEY

∽ = chain (ch)

✕ = single crochet (sc)

T = half double crochet (hdc)

Ŧ = double crochet (dc)

Stitch Diagram

Handle Stitch Diagram

Bag

Ch 61.

Row 1 (RS): Sc in 2nd ch from hook, sc in each ch across, turn—60 sts.

Row 2: Ch 1, sc in first 2 sc, * ch 10, skip 4 sc, sc in next 4 sc; repeat from * across, sc in last 2 sts, turn.

Row 3: Ch 1, sc in first 2 sts, * ch 5, 2 sc in next loop, ch 5, skip 1 sc, sc in next 2 sc; repeat from * across; end with ch 5, sc in last 2 sts, turn.

Row 4: Ch 3, dc in first st, ch 5, * sc in next loop, sc in next 2 sc, sc in next loop, ch 10; repeat from * across, ending with ch 5, dc in last 2 sts, turn.

Row 5: Ch 1, sc in first 2 sts, * ch 5, skip sc, sc in next 2 sc, ch 5, 2 sc in next loop; repeat from * across, ending with ch 5, sc in last 2 sts, turn.

Row 6: Ch 3, dc in first st, ch 10, skip ch-5 and sc group, * sc in next loop, sc in next 2 sc, sc in next loop, ch 10; repeat from * across, dc in last 2 sts, turn.

Repeat Rows 3-6 until piece measures 26" (66cm), ending with Row 5.

Next Row: Ch 1, sc in next 2 sts, ch 4, skip ch-5 and 2 sc, * sc in next loop, sc in next 2 sts, sc in next loop, ch 4; repeat from * across, turn.

Last Row: Ch 1, sc in first st, sc in each st across. Fasten off.

Handles

Make 2.

Ch 80.

Next row: Hdc in 3rd ch from hook, hdc in each ch across. Fasten off.

Finishing

Fold bag in half with RS facing and sew side seams. Sew handles to top of bag. Weave in ends.

"Shell Stripe" Mat and Glass Jackets A-511

Mat measures about 9 inches in diameter

The amount of material given is sufficient for 6 Glass Jackets and 1 Mat.

COATS & CLARK'S "O.N.T." RUG YARN: 2 skeins of No. 60 Straw.

COATS & CLARK'S "O.N.T." "SPEED-CRO-SHEEN" MERCERIZED COTTON: 1 ball of No. 126 Spanish Red.

Milwards Steel Crochet Hook No. 2/0 (double zero).

Crochet Hook Size H.

GAUGE: 7 sc = 2 inches; 4 rnds = 1 inch.

MAT . . . Starting at center with Straw and Size H hook, ch 4. Join with sl st to

spaced—48 sc at end of 8th rnd. Sl st in next sc. Break off and fasten.

Insertion: Using Red and No. 2/0 hook, attach thread to any sc, sc in same sc, * skip next sc, in next sc make 3 dc—shell made; skip next sc, sc in next sc. Repeat from * around, ending with a shell in next-to-last sc. Join with sl st to first sc. Break off and fasten.

Border: 1st rnd: Using Straw and Size H hook, attach yarn to the ch-1 sp of any shell, sc in same sp, * ch 5, sc in sp of next shell. Repeat from * around, ending with ch 5, sc in first sc. 2nd rnd: Sc in

---

"Zig Zag" Hot Plate Mat and Pot Holder A-510

Illustrated on Page 29

COATS & CLARK'S "O.N.T." RUG YARN: 2 skeins of No. 1 White and 1 skein of No. 76 Robinette.

Crochet Hook Size G.

GAUGE: 7 sts = 2 inches; 4 rows = 1 inch.

HOT PLATE MAT . . . With Robinette, ch 37 to measure 10½ inches (7 ch sts to 2 inches). 1st row: Sc in 2nd ch from hook and in each ch across. Drop Robinette, attach White. Ch 1, turn. 2nd row: With White sc in first sc, * sc in same ch where each of next 2 sc were made, ch 2, skip the 2 sc covered by the 2 sc just made and following 2 sc. Repeat from * across, ending with skip the 2 sc covered by the 2 sc just made, sc in last sc. Ch 1, turn. 3rd row: Sc in first sc, * ch 2, skip next 2 sc, working over the ch-2, sc in each of next 2 sc 1 row below—2 long sc made. Repeat from * across to within last 3 sts, ch 2, skip next 2 sc in last sc. Drop White, pick up Robinette. Ch 1, turn. 4th row: Sc in first sc, long sc in each of next 2 long sc 1 row below. * ch 2, skip next 2 sc, long sc, long sc in each of next 2 long sc 1 row below. Repeat from * across to within last sc. Ch 1, turn. 5th row: Sc in first sc, * ch 2, skip next 2 long sc, long sc in each of next 2 long sc 1 row below. Repeat from * across to within last 3 sts, ch 2, skip next 2 long sc in last sc. Change color. Ch 1, turn. Repeat 4th and 5th rows al-

ternately, changing color at end of every uneven row until 39 rows have been completed. Drop White, pick up Robinette and turn. Last row: Sl st in first sc, long sc in each of next 2 long sc 1 row below, * sl st in next 2 long sc, long sc in each of next 2 long sc 1 row below. Repeat from * across, ending with sl st in last st. Break off and fasten.

Border: 1st rnd: Pick up White, make 3 sc in first sl st, sc in next 2 long sc, * sc in next 2 sts, sc in next 2 long sc. Repeat from * across to within last sl st, sc in last sl st, being careful to keep work flat. Sc closely along next side edge; now working along opposite side of starting chain, make 3 sc in last ch, sc in each ch across, making 3 sc in last ch; sc closely along next side edge to correspond with opposite side. Join with sl st to first sc. Turn. 2nd rnd: Sl st in each sc around. Join. Break off and fasten.

POT HOLDER . . . With Robinette ch 21 to measure 6 inches. Work in pattern as for Hot Plate Mat until 23 rows have been completed. Last row: Repeat last row of Hot Plate Mat.

Border: Work as for Border of Hot Plate Mat. Do not break off at end of last rnd.

LOOP . . . Ch 10, sl st in second sl st of 2nd rnd; turn and sl st in each ch. Join to last sl st of last rnd. Break off and fasten. Press through a damp cloth.

A-511 Continued from page 30

GLASS JACKET . . . Work as for Mat until the 4th rnd has been completed. Next rnd: Work as before, increasing 4 sc

Insertion: Work same as on Mat.

Border: 1st rnd: Using Straw and Size H

Chapter Two

Entertaining Tables

Set a pleasing table with some modern remakes of lacy and colorful ideas resurrected from the past. You'll find placemats with matching glass holders, sophisticated scalloped placemats and clever mats with watermelon and pineapple motifs. The crocus doily is a beautiful classic that has been updated in soft, smooth bamboo thread.

Shell Stripe Placemat & Glass Holders

If you thought that cup cozies were a relatively new idea, you were mistaken. The idea was around in the 1950s for iced tea (or high ball) glasses. These holders go around the bottom of the glass, so they are actually more like portable coasters for your party potables.

Adapted by Tracie Barrett

SIZES: *One size*

FINISHED MEASUREMENTS:

MAT: *15" (38cm) in diameter*

GLASS HOLDERS: *2½" (6cm) in diameter, 2" (5cm) tall*

YARN:

1 skein Red Heart® Super Saver® (acrylic, 364 yds [333m] per 7 oz skein) in each of colors #0624 Tea Leaf (A) and #0365 Coffee (B)

HOOK: *Size J (6mm) and I (5.5mm) crochet hooks*

NOTIONS:

Stitch marker

Yarn needle

GAUGE: *Rounds 1-7 = 4" (10cm) in pattern using larger hook*

SPECIAL STITCH:

Shell Stitch: (2 dc, ch 1, 2 dc) in same stitch

"Shell Stripe" Mat and Glass Jackets A-511

Mat measures about 9 inches in diameter

The amount of material given is sufficient for 6 Glass Jackets and 1 Mat.

COATS & CLARK'S "O.N.T." RUG YARN: 2 skeins of No. 60 Straw.

COATS & CLARK'S O.N.T. "SPEED-CRO-SHEEN" MERCERIZED COTTON: 1 ball of No. 126 Spanish Red.

Milwards Steel Crochet Hook No. 2/0 (double zero).

Crochet Hook Size H.

GAUGE: 7 sc = 2 inches; 4 rnds = 1 inch.

MAT . . . Starting at center with Straw and Size H hook, ch 4. Join with sl st to form ring. **1st rnd:** 6 sc in ring. **2nd rnd:** 2 sc in each sc around. **3rd rnd:** (Sc in next sc, 2 sc in next sc—1 sc increased) 6 times. **4th rnd:** (Sc in next 2 sc, 2 sc in next sc) 6 times. **5th through 8th rnd:** Sc in each sc around, increasing 6 sc evenly

spaced—48 sc at end of 8th rnd. Sl st in next sc. Break off and fasten.

Insertion: Using Red and No. 2/0 hook, attach thread to any sc, sc in same sc, * skip next sc, in next sc make 3 dc, ch 1 and 3 dc—shell made; skip next sc, sc in next sc. Repeat from * around, ending with a shell in next-to-last sc. Join with sl st to first sc. Break off and fasten.

Border: **1st rnd:** Using Straw and Size H hook, attach yarn to the ch-1 sp of any shell, sc in same sp, * ch 5, sc in sp of next shell. Repeat from * around, ending with ch 5, sc in first sc. **2nd rnd:** Sc in each sc and in each ch around—72 sc. **Next 5 rnds:** Repeat 5th rnd of Mat. At end of last rnd, sl st in next sc. Turn. **Next rnd:** With wrong side facing, sl st in each sc around. Join. Break off and fasten. Press lightly.

Continued on page 31

[30]

NOTE: *Do not join rounds unless indicated.*

Shell Stripe Placemat & Glass Holders

Placemat

Round 1: Using larger hook and A, ch 2, work 6 sc in 2nd ch from hook, place marker in last st (move marker to end of each following round as work progresses).

Round 2: 2 sc in each st around—12 sc.

Round 3: *Sc in next sc, 2 sc in next sc; repeat from * around—18 sc.

Round 4: *Sc in next 2 sc, 2 sc in next sc; repeat from * around—24 sc.

Rounds 5-8: Work increases in each round as established—48 sc in last round. On final round, join with slip st in first sc. Fasten off.

Round 9: Join B with sc in any st, skip next sc, [shell in next sc, skip next sc, sc in next sc, skip next sc] 11 times, shell in next sc, skip next sc, join with slip st in first sc. Fasten off.

Round 10: Join A with sc in any ch-1 space from previous round, ch 5, *sc in next ch-1 space, ch 5; repeat from * around, sc in first sc, place marker in this st.

Round 11: Sc in each ch and stitch around—72 sc.

Round 12: *Sc in next 8 sc, 2 sc in next st; repeat from * around—80 sc.

Round 13: *Sc in next 9 sc, 2 sc in next st; repeat from * around—88 sc.

Rounds 14-15: Work increases in each round as established—104 sc in last round. Fasten off.

Round 16: Join B with sc in any st, skip next sc, [shell in next sc, skip next sc, sc in next sc, skip next sc] 25 times, shell in next sc, skip next sc, join with slip st in first sc. Fasten off.

Round 17: Join A with sc in any ch-1 space, ch 4, *sc in next ch-1 space, ch 4; repeat from * around, sc in first sc, place marker in this st.

Round 18: Sc in each ch and stitch around—130 sc.

Round 19: *Sc in next 12 sc, 2 sc in next st; repeat from * around—140 sc.

Rounds 20-22: Work increases in each round as established—170 sc in last round.

Rounds 23-24: Sc in each st around. On last round, join with slip st in first st. Turn.

Round 25: Slip st into each sc around and join. Fasten off.

Glass Holder

Rounds 1-4: Using smaller hook, work as for Mat.

Round 5: *Sc in next 5 sc, 2 sc in next sc; repeat from * around, join with slip st in first st—28 sc.

Round 6: Ch 1, sc in back loop only of same st as joining and each st around, join with slip st in first st.

Round 7: Ch 1, sc in both loops of each st around. Join with slip st in first st. Fasten off.

Round 8: Join B with sc in any stitch, skip next sc, [shell in next sc, skip next sc, sc in next sc, skip next sc] 6 times, shell in next sc, skip next sc, join with slip st in first sc. Fasten off.

Round 9: Join A with sc in any ch-1 space from previous round, ch 3, *sc in next ch-1 space, ch 3; repeat from * around, sc in first sc, place marker in this st.

Round 10: Sc in each st and ch around.

Round 11: Sc in each st around, join with slip st in first sc. Fasten off.

Finishing
Weave in ends. Block lightly.

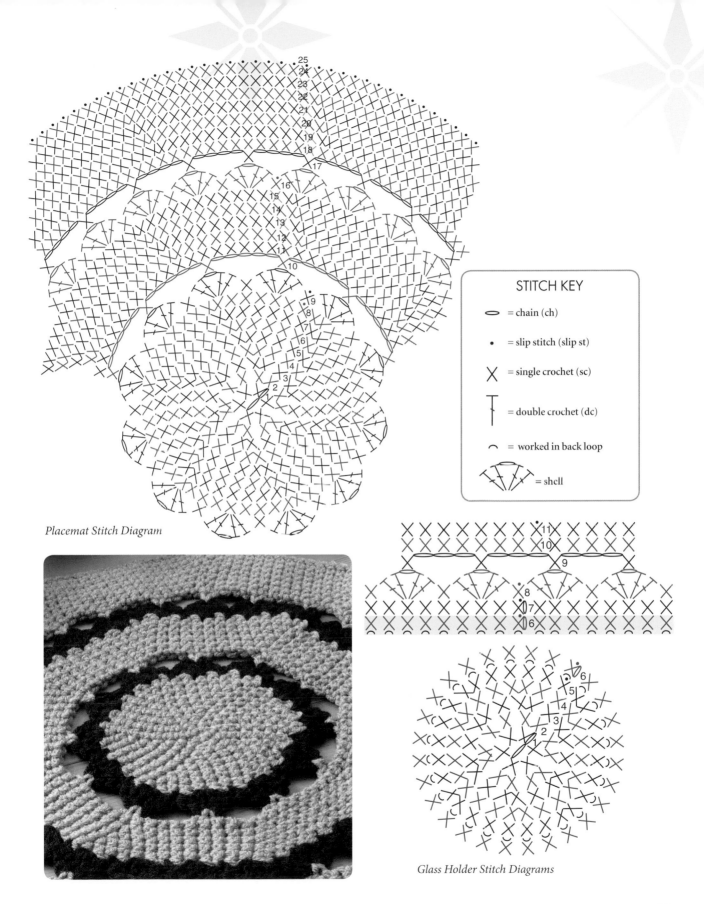

STITCH KEY

◯ = chain (ch)

• = slip stitch (slip st)

✕ = single crochet (sc)

T = double crochet (dc)

⌒ = worked in back loop

= shell

Placemat Stitch Diagram

Glass Holder Stitch Diagrams

Watermelon Placemat & Serving Mat

In their original 1954 presentation, these mats were billed as best sellers for a "Carnival of Quick Tricks." "So step right up, don't waste another minute, Ladies. Pick up your hooks and start one of these mats." Proving that tastes don't change much, these will make you want to take up your hooks.

Adapted by
Sharon Mann

Oval Placemat

SIZES: *One size*

FINISHED MEASUREMENTS : *12" × 19" (30cm × 48cm)*

THREAD:

2 balls Aunt Lydia's® Classic Crochet Thread, size 10 (mercerized cotton, 350 yds [320m] per 2.3 oz ball) in each of colors #0493 French Rose (A), #0001 White (B), #0428 Mint Green (C), #0661 Frosty Green (D)

1 ball Aunt Lydia's® Classic Crochet Thread, size 10 (mercerized cotton, 350 yds [320m] per 2.3 oz ball) in color #0012 Black (E)

HOOK: *Size 6 (1.8mm) steel crochet hook*

NOTIONS: *Yarn needle*

GAUGE: *32 sts and 14 rows = 4" (10cm) with thread held double*

Round Serving Mat

SIZES: *One size*

FINISHED MEASUREMENTS: *14" (36cm) in diameter*

THREAD:

2 balls Aunt Lydia's® Classic Crochet Thread, size 10 (mercerized cotton, 350 yds [320m] per 2.3 oz ball) in each of colors #0493 French Rose (A), #0001 White (B), #0428 Mint Green (C), #0661 Frosty Green (D)

1 ball Aunt Lydia's® Classic Crochet Thread, size 10 (mercerized cotton, 350 yds [320m] per 2.3 oz ball) in color #0012 Black (E)

HOOK: *Size 6 (1.8mm) steel crochet hook*

NOTIONS: *Yarn needle*

GAUGE: *32 sts and 14 rows = 4" (10cm) with thread held double*

Watermelon Placemat & Plate Mat

Oval Placemat

With A held double, make a chain 5½" (14cm) long.

Round 1: 5 sc in 2nd ch from hook, sc in each ch across, 5 sc in last ch, sc across the opposite side of ch, join with slip st in first sc.

Round 2: Ch 3, dc in same space, 2 dc in next 5 sts, dc in each st across, inc 6 sts across rounded end, dc in each st across opposite side, join with slip st in top of ch-3.

Round 3: Ch 1, sc in each st around, inc 5 sts evenly at rounded ends.

Round 4: Ch 3, dc in each st around, inc 6 sts evenly at rounded ends.

Rounds 5-18: Repeat Rounds 3 and 4. Fasten off.

Round 19: Join B with slip st, sc in same space as slip st, sc in each st around, join with slip st in first sc.

Round 20: Ch 3, dc in next st, dc in each st around, join with slip st in top of ch-3. Fasten off.

Round 21: Join C, repeat Round 3.

Round 22: Ch 1, sc in same space as slip st, sc in each st around, join with slip st in first sc. Fasten off.

Round 23: Join D, repeat Round 3.

Round 24: Sc in same space as slip st, sc in each st around, join with slip st in first sc.

Round 25: Ch 3, dc in each st around, join with slip st in top of ch-3. Fasten off.

Round 26: With B, join with slip st, *ch 5, skip 3 sts, sc in next st; repeat from * around, join with slip st in first st.

Round 27: Slip st across first 3 ch of loop, *ch 5, sc in next loop; repeat from * around to last loop, join with slip st in first st. Fasten off.

Finishing

With E, embroider ¼" (6mm) seeds (4 sts makes 1 seed) around the center of the Mat. Weave in ends. Steam block with iron.

Round Serving Mat

With A held double, ch 2.

Round 1: 7 sc in 2nd ch from hook, join with slip st in first sc.

Round 2: Ch 3, 2 dc in same st, 3 dc in each sc around, join with slip st in top of ch-3—21 dc.

Round 3: Ch 1, 2 sc in same space (inc made), *sc in next 2 sts, 2 sc in next st; repeat from * around, join with slip st in first sc—28 sc.

Round 4: Ch 3, *2 dc in next st (inc made), dc in next st; repeat from * around, join with slip st in top of ch-3—42 dc.

Round 5: Ch 1, sc in same space as slip st, sc in each st, inc 7 sc evenly around, join with slip st in first sc—49 sc.

Round 6: Ch 3, dc in each st, inc 14 sts evenly around, join with slip st in top of ch-3—63 dc.

Rounds 7-22: Repeat Rounds 5 and 6—231 dc. Fasten off.

Round 23: Join B with slip st, sc in same space, sc in each st around, join with slip st in first sc.

Round 24: Ch 3, dc in next st, dc in each st around, join with slip st in top of ch-3. Fasten off.

Round 25: Join C with slip st, repeat Round 23. Fasten off.

Round 26: Repeat Round 5—238 sc.

Rounds 27–28: Join D with slip st, repeat Round 5—252 sc.

Round 29: Ch 3, dc in each st around, join with slip st in top of ch-3. Fasten off.

Round 30: Join B with slip st, *ch 5, skip 3 sts, sc in next st; repeat from * around, join with slip st in first st.

Round 31: Slip st across first 3 ch of loop, *ch 5, sc in next loop; repeat from * around to last loop, join with slip st in first st. Fasten off.

Finishing

With E, embroider ¼" (6mm) seeds (4 sts makes 1 seed) around the center of the Mat. Weave in ends. Steam block with iron.

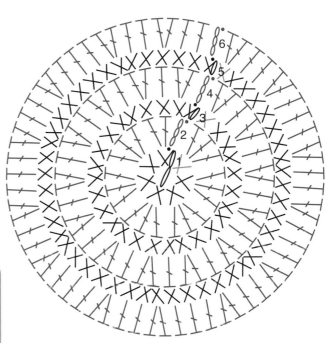

Rounds 1-6 Round Mat Stitch Diagram

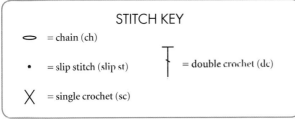

STITCH KEY

⬭ = chain (ch)

• = slip stitch (slip st)

⊤ = double crochet (dc)

✕ = single crochet (sc)

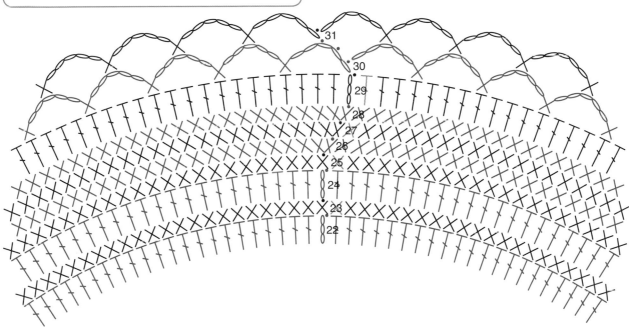

Rounds 22-31 Round Mat Stitch Diagram

Pineapple Hot Plate Mat

Recycle your bottle caps—the kind that have crimped edges and need a bottle opener to remove them from the bottle. This technique of covering bottle caps was popular in the mid 20th century. The pineapple is a traditional symbol to welcome guests into the home. Imagine this mat being used for serving pineapple upside-down cake!

Adapted by Tracie Barrett

Sizes: *One size*

Finished Measurements: *10″ × 18″ (25cm × 46cm)*

Thread:

2 balls Aunt Lydia's® Classic Crochet Thread, size 10 (mercerized cotton, 350 yds [320m] per 2 oz ball) in color #422 Golden Yellow (A)

1 ball Aunt Lydia's® Classic Crochet Thread, size 10 (mercerized cotton, 350 yds [320m] per 2 oz ball) in color #449 Forest Green (B)

Hook: *Size D (3.25mm) crochet hook*

Notions:

Stitch marker

Yarn needle

52 metal bottle caps

Gauge: *Rounds 1 & 2= 1″ (3cm) in pattern*

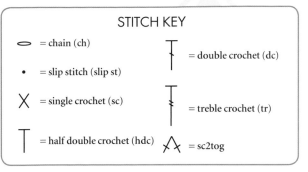

STITCH KEY

⬯ = chain (ch)

• = slip stitch (slip st)

✕ = single crochet (sc)

T = half double crochet (hdc)

T = double crochet (dc)

‡ = treble crochet (tr)

⋏ = sc2tog

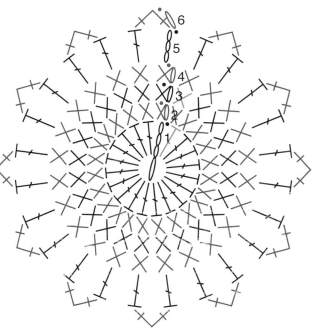

Leaf Stitch Diagram

SPECIAL ABBREVIATION:

Sc2tog: Insert hook into next stitch, pull up a loop, insert hook into next stitch, pull up a loop, yo, pull through all 3 loops on hook.

NOTE: *Hold thread double throughout unless otherwise stated. Do not join rounds unless stated.*

Plate Mat

Cap Cover

Make 54.

With 2 strands of A held double, ch 4 (ch 3 counts as dc here and throughout).

Round 1: Work 19 dc in 4th ch from hook. Join to top of starting ch—20 dc.

Round 2: Ch 1, sc in ch sp and next 3 dc, 2 sc in next dc, *sc in next 4 dc, 2 sc in next dc; repeat from * around—24 sc.

Rounds 3–4: Ch1, sc in each st around, join with slip st in first sc.

Round 5: Ch 3, dc in each st around, join with slip st.

Round 6: Ch 1, sc2tog around, inserting cap into cover halfway around. Join with slip st to first st and fasten off, leaving a 6" (15cm) tail. With needle, run thread in and out of all sts, gather tightly and knot securely. Use tail to attach caps together as shown.

Leaf

Make 10.

Cap Cover Stitch Diagram

With 2 strands of B held double, ch 28.

Row 1: Sc in 2nd ch from hook, hdc in next 5 ch, dc in next 5 ch, tr in next 5 ch, dc in next 5 ch, hdc in next 5 ch, sc in last ch. Do not turn.

Round 2: Working on other side of foundation ch, sc in each ch across, work 3 sc in last ch at tip, continue around and sc in next 27 sts back towards base of leaf. Join. Fasten off.

Finishing

Place 2 leaves together with WS facing. Using 1 strand of B and working through both layers, join thread with a slip st into base of leaf. Slip st layers together and fasten off at end of base, leaving a long tail for sewing. Repeat with remaining leaves.

Sew caps together as pictured. Using tails from leaves, sew leaves together and to top of mat.

Scalloped Placemat

The original scallops were crocheted in rows of chartreuse green and hunter's green. We opted to remake it in a coordinating print and solid in more sophisticated tones of copper and aspen greens.

Adapted by Mary Ann Frits

SIZES: *One size*

FINISHED MEASUREMENTS: *14″ × 19″ (36cm × 48cm)*

THREAD:

2 balls Aunt Lydia's® Fashion Crochet Thread, size 3 (mercerized cotton, 150 yds [137m] per 2.2 oz ball) in each of colors #935 Aspen Print (A), #310 Copper Mist (B)

HOOK: *Size F (3.75mm) crochet hook*

NOTIONS: *Yarn needle*

GAUGE: *20 sts = 4″ (10cm)*

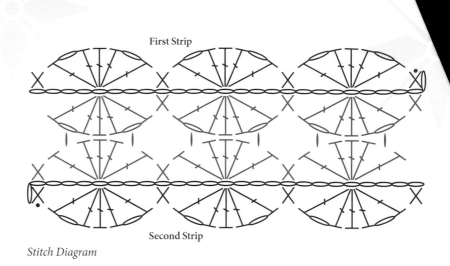

First Strip

Second Strip

Stitch Diagram

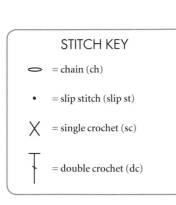

STITCH KEY

⬯ = chain (ch)

• = slip stitch (slip st)

✗ = single crochet (sc)

⊤ = double crochet (dc)

Placemat

First Strip

With A, ch 98, sc in 2nd ch from hook, * skip next 3 ch, (dc, ch 1, 3 dc, ch 1, dc) in next ch (scallop made), skip next 3 ch, sc in next ch; repeat from * across. Working in unused loops on opposite side of foundation ch, ** (dc, ch 1, 3 dc, ch 1, dc) in unused loop at base of next scallop (scallop made), sc in unused loop at base of next sc; repeat from ** across; join with slip st in first sc. Fasten off.

Second Strip

With B, ch 98, sc in 2nd ch from hook, * skip next 3 ch, (dc, ch 1, 3 dc, ch 1, dc) in next ch (scallop made), skip next 3 ch, sc in next ch; repeat from * across. Working in unused loops on opposite side of foundation ch, ** dc in unused loop at base of next scallop, hold last strip made with WS facing, slip st in first ch-1 space of corresponding scallop on completed strip, 3 dc in same space on working strip, slip st in next ch-1 space on completed strip, dc in same space on working strip (joined scallop made), sc in unused loop at base of next sc; repeat from ** across; join with slip st in first sc. Fasten off.

Work 19 additional strips, alternating colors and join them as for Second Strip.

Finishing

Weave in ends.

47

Early Crocus Doily

Although the original was gorgeous, it was crocheted and then stiffened. Our modern day version is crocheted with soft, smooth bamboo thread so it is soft and natural to the touch. But of course, you can use whatever thread you prefer.

Adapted by Nazanin Fard

SIZES: *One size*

FINISHED MEASUREMENTS: *18″ (46cm) in diameter*

THREAD:

1 ball Aunt Lydia's® Bamboo Crochet Thread, size 10 (viscose from bamboo, 300 yd (274 m) per 1.6 oz ball) in color #0320 Mushroom

HOOK: *Size 7 (1.65mm) steel crochet hook*

NOTIONS: *Yarn needle*

GAUGE: *Rounds 1-3 = 1″ (3cm)*

Doily

Ch 10. Join with a slip st to make a ring.

Round 1: Ch 1, 24 sc in ring, join with a slip st.

Round 2: Beg-tr cluster, ch 5, * skip next sc, 4-tr cluster in next sc, ch 5; repeat from * around, end with a slip st in top of beg-tr cluster.

Round 3: Beg-shell on top of beg-cluster, ch 3, sc in 3rd ch from previous round, ch 3, * shell on top of next cluster, ch 3, sc in 3rd ch from previous round, ch 3; repeat from * around, end with a slip st in top of beg-cluster.

Round 4: Slip st in next dc, slip st in ch-2 space, beg-shell in ch-2 space, * ch 5, shell in next shell; repeat from * around, end with ch 5, slip st in 3rd ch.

Round 5: Slip st in next dc, slip st in ch-2 space, beg-shell in ch-2 space, ch 4, sc in 3rd ch from previous round, * ch 4, shell in next shell, ch 4, sc in 3rd ch from previous round; repeat from * around, end with ch 4, slip st in 3rd ch.

Round 6: Slip st in next dc, slip st in ch-2 space, beg-shell in ch-2 space, * ch 7, shell in next shell; repeat from * around, end with ch 7, slip st in 3rd ch.

Round 7: Slip st in next dc, slip st in ch-2 space, big beg-shell in ch-2 space, ch 5, sc in 4th ch from previous round, * ch 4, big shell in next shell, ch 4, sc in 4th ch from previous round; repeat from * around, end with ch 4, slip st in 3rd ch.

Round 8: Slip st in next dc, slip st in ch-2 space, beg-dtr cluster in next ch-4 space, * [ch 5, 4-dtr cluster] in same ch-4 space 3 times, 4-dtr cluster in next ch-4 space; repeat from * around, end with a slip st in top of beg-cluster.

Round 9: Slip st in next 2 ch, sc in same ch-space, * ch 5, sc in same ch-space, [ch 7, sc in next ch-space] twice; repeat from * around, ending with ch 3, tr in first sc instead of ch 7.

Round 10: * Ch 3, shell in next ch-5 space, ch 3, sc in next ch-7 space, ch 7, sc in next ch-7 space, ch 3;

SPECIAL ABBREVIATIONS:

Beg-tr cluster: Ch 4, * yo hook twice, insert hook through space, pull thread through, [pull thread through 2 loops on hook] twice; repeat from * a total of 3 times, yo hook, pull thread through all loops on hook.

4-tr cluster: * Yo hook twice, insert hook through space, pull thread through, [pull thread through 2 loops on hook] twice; repeat from * a total of 4 times, yo hook, pull thread through all loops on hook.

Beg-dtr cluster: Ch 5, * yo hook 3 times, insert hook through space, pull thread through, [pull thread through 2 loops on hook] 3 times; repeat from * a total of 3 times, yo hook, pull thread through all loops on hook.

4-dtr cluster: * Yo hook 3 times, insert hook through space, pull thread through, [pull thread through 2 loops on hook] 3 times; repeat from * a total of 4 times, yo hook, pull thread through all loops on hook.

Beg-shell: Ch 3, dc in same space, ch 2, 2 dc in same space.

Shell: 2 dc in next space, ch 2, 2 dc in same space.

Big Beg-shell: Ch 3, dc in same space, ch 4, 2 dc in same space.

Big Shell: 2 dc in next space, ch 4, 2 dc in same space.

repeat from * around, end with ch 3, tr on top of tr of previous round.

Round 11: * Ch 5, shell in next shell, ch 5, sc in next ch-7 space; repeat from * around.

Round 12: Slip st in each of next ch 5, slip st in each of next 2 dc, slip st in ch-2 space, beg-shell in ch-2 space, * ch 9, shell in next shell; repeat from * around, end with ch 9, slip st in 3rd ch.

Round 13: Slip st in next dc, slip st in next ch-2 space, beg-shell in next shell, * ch 3, sc in next ch-9 space, ch 7, sc in same ch-9 space, ch 3, shell in next shell; repeat from * around, end with ch 3, sc in next ch-9 space, ch 7, sc in same ch-9 space, ch 3, slip st in 3rd ch.

Early Crocus Doily

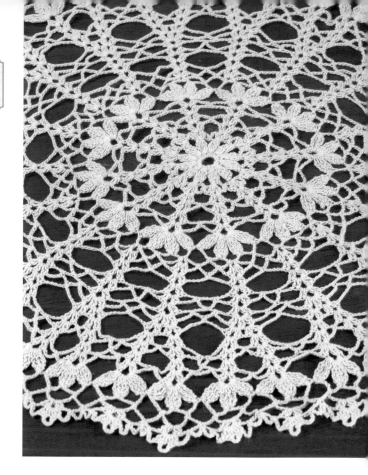

Round 14: Slip st in next dc, slip st in next ch-2 space, beg-shell in next shell, * ch 5, sc in next ch-7 space, ch 5, shell in next shell; repeat from * around.

Round 15: Slip st in next dc, slip st in next ch-2 space, beg-shell in next shell, * ch 2, 2 dc in same ch-space, ch 5, sc in next ch-5 space, ch 5, sc in next ch-5 space, ch 5, shell in next shell; repeat from * around.

Round 16: Slip st in next dc, slip st in next ch-2 space, beg-shell in next shell, * ch 1, shell in next ch-2 space, ch 5, skip next ch-5 space, sc in next ch-5 space, ch 5, shell in next shell; repeat from * around, end with ch 5, skip next ch-5 space, sc in next ch-5 space, ch 5, slip st in 3rd ch.

Round 17: Slip st in next dc, slip st in next ch-2 space, beg-shell in next shell, * ch 3, shell in next shell, ch 11, shell in next shell; repeat from * around, end with ch 11, slip st in 3rd ch.

Round 18: Slip st in next dc, slip st in next ch-2 space, beg-shell in next shell, * ch 3, sc in ch-3-space, ch 3, shell in next shell, (ch 3, sc, ch 5, sc) in ch-11 space, ch 3, shell in next shell; repeat from * around, end with (ch 3, sc, ch 5, sc) in ch-11 space, ch 3, slip st in 3rd ch.

Round 19: Slip st in next dc, slip st in next ch-2 space, beg-shell in next shell, * ch 9, shell in next shell, ch 5, sc in ch-5 space, ch 5, shell in next shell; repeat from * around, end with ch 5, sc in ch-5 space, ch 5, slip st in 3rd ch.

Round 20: Slip st in next dc, slip st in next ch-2 space, big beg-shell in next shell, * ch 5, sc in ch-9 space, ch 5, big shell in next shell, ch 3, sc in next ch-5 space, ch 5, sc in next ch-5 space, ch 3, big shell in next shell; repeat from * around, end with

ch 3, sc in next ch-5 space, ch 5, sc in next ch-5 space, ch 3, slip st in 3rd ch.

Round 21: Slip st in next dc, slip st in next ch-2 space, beg dtr-cluster in next ch-4 space, * [ch 7, 4 dtr-cluster in same ch-4 space] twice, 4 dtr-cluster in next ch-4 space; repeat from * around, end with a slip st in top of first 4 dtr-cluster.

Round 22: Ch 1, [slip st in next ch] 5 times, * ch 9, sc in next ch-9 space; repeat from * around, end with ch 4, tr in first ch.

Round 23: * Ch 5, shell in next ch-9 space, ch 5, sc in next ch-9 space; repeat from * around, end with ch 5, slip st in first ch.

Round 24: * Ch 5, sc in next ch-5 space, ch 5, (3 dc, ch 5, 3 dc) in next shell, ch 5, sc in next ch-5 space; repeat from * around, end with ch 5, slip st in first ch. Fasten off.

Finishing
Weave in ends. Block.

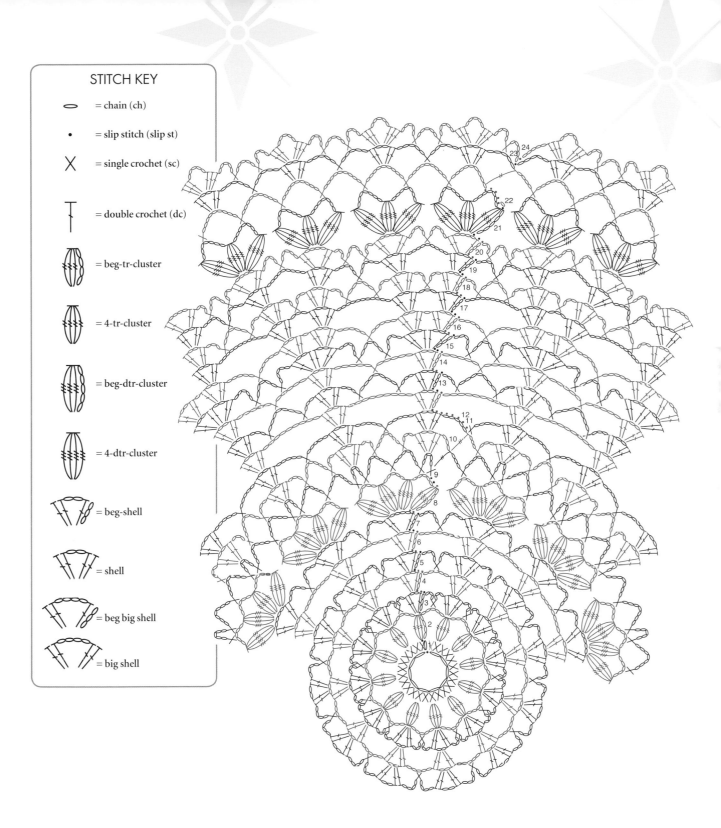

STITCH KEY

- ⬯ = chain (ch)
- • = slip stitch (slip st)
- ✕ = single crochet (sc)
- ⊤ = double crochet (dc)
- = beg-tr-cluster
- = 4-tr-cluster
- = beg-dtr-cluster
- = 4-dtr-cluster
- = beg-shell
- = shell
- = beg big shell
- = big shell

Elegant Gifts . . . for Housewarming Parties

Directions for A-540 on Page 20 . . . A-541 on Page 34

Crocheted Edging A-539

J. & P. COATS "BIG BALL" BEST SIX CORD
MERCERIZED CROCHET, Size 30; or

CLARK'S "BIG BALL" MERCERIZED CROCHET,
Size 30: 1 ball of any color.

Milwards Steel Crochet Hook No. 10.

1 guest towel.

Edging measures 1 inch wide

Starting at heading edge, make a chain
2 inches longer than desired length, having 12 ch to 1 inch. **1st row:** Dc in 4th ch
from hook and in each ch across for desired length, having a number of dc di-
visible by 8 plus 5 (counting the first 3 ch
as 1 dc). Cut off any remaining chain.
Ch 1, turn. **2nd row:** In first dc make sc,
ch 3 and 3 dc; skip next 3 dc, 3 dc in
next dc, * skip next 3 dc, in next dc
make sc, ch 3 and 3 dc; skip next 3 dc,
3 dc in next dc. Repeat from * across.
Ch 1, turn. **3rd row:** Skip first dc, *in next
dc make sc, dc, ch 3, dc and sc—shell
made,* shell in next ch-3 sp, skip next sc
and following dc, shell in next dc. Repeat
from * across, ending with shell in last
ch-3 sp. Ch 1, turn. **4th row:** Sl st in
first 2 sts; in first shell sp make dc, ch 6
and dc; * in first shell sp make dc, ch 3
and dc—V st made. Repeat from * across.
Ch 1, turn. **5th row:** In first V-st sp make
sc, ch 3 and sc; * in 2nd dc of same V st
make sc, ch 3 and sc; in next V-st sp make
sc, ch 3 and sc. Repeat from * across.
Press lightly. Sew in place as shown

A-539

A-540

A-541

CLARK'S O.N.T. · J.&P. COATS   BATHROOM BEAUTIES   BOOK No. 265

Bathroom Beauties

DECORATIVE CROCHET FOR BATH TOWELS · GUEST TOWELS · FACE CLOTHS

10¢

Chapter Three

Bed & Bath Décor

There's no need to go searching through antique stores for old-fashioned charm in the perfect color accents for your room. This chapter offers ideas that you can recreate in your favorite color scheme. You'll love these rugs, lacy edgings for pillow cases, water lily appliqués and lace for bath towels.

Circular Rug

The original designer made this rug using just one color. But we couldn't resist combining four favorite yarn colors for a striped version. This rug is perfect for a bedroom or kid's room.

*Adapted by
Darla Sims*

SIZES: *One size*

FINISHED MEASUREMENT: *34"
(86cm) in diameter*

YARN:

*2 skeins Red Heart® Super Saver®
(acrylic, 364 yds [333m] per 7 oz
skein) in each of colors #505 Aruba
Sea (A), #661 Frosty Green (C),
#530 Orchid (D)*

*2 skeins Red Heart® Super Saver®
Prints (acrylic, 244 yds [233m] per
5 oz skein) in color #310 Monet
Print (B)*

HOOK: *Size K (7mm) crochet hook*

NOTIONS: *Yarn needle*

GAUGE: *10 sts and 6 rows = 4"
(10cm) with yarn held double*

SPECIAL STITCH:

Puff: *[Yo, pull up loop] 3 times,
yo, pull yarn though all 7 loops on
hook.*

NOTE: *Hold 2 strands of yarn
together throughout.
1 stitch = 1 sc OR 1 ch-1 space.*

Circular Rug

Rug

Round 1 (RS): With 2 strands of A held together, ch 2, work 12 sc in 2nd ch from hook, join.

Round 2: (Ch 2, [yo, pull up loop] twice, yo, pull yarn though all 5 loops on hook – beg Puff made), ch 1, * work (Puff, ch 1) in next st; repeat from * around; join to top of beg Puff—12 Puffs.

Round 3: Ch 1, sc in same st, 2 sc in next st, *sc in next st, 2 sc in next st; repeat from * around. Fasten off—36 sts.

Round 4: Join B in same st, work beg Puff, ch 1, * skip next sc, (Puff, ch 1) in next sc; repeat from * around, join to top of beg Puff—18 Puffs.

Round 5: Ch 1, sc in same st, 2 sc in next st, * sc in next st, 2 sc in next st; repeat from * around, join—54 sts.

Round 6: Repeat Round 4—27 Puffs.

Round 7: Ch 1, sc in same st, sc in next st, 2 sc in next st, * sc in next 2 sts, 2 sc in next st; repeat from * around, join—72 sts.

Round 8: Repeat Round 4—36 Puffs.

Round 9: Ch 1, sc in same st, sc in next 2 sts, 2 sc in next st, * sc in next 3 sts, 2 sc in next st; repeat from * around, join.

Round 10: Repeat Round 4—45 Puffs.

Round 11: Ch 1, sc in same st, sc in next 3 sts, 2 sc in next st, * sc in next 4 sts, 2 sc in next st; repeat from * around.

Round 12: Repeat Round 4—54 Puffs.

Round 13: Ch 1, sc in same st, sc in next 4 sts, 2 sc in next st, *sc in next 5 sts, 2 sc in next st; repeat from * around.

Round 14: Repeat Round 4—63 Puffs.

Round 15: Ch 1, sc in same st, sc in next 5 sts, 2 sc in next st, * sc in next 6 sts, 2 sc in next st; repeat from * around.

Round 16: Repeat Round 4—72 Puffs.

Round 17: Ch 1, sc in same st, sc in next 6 sts, 2 sc in next st, * sc in next 7 sts, 2 sc in next st; repeat from * around—162 sts.

Round 18: Repeat Round 4—81 Puffs.

Round 19: Ch 1, sc in same st, sc in next 7 sts, 2 sc in next st, * sc in next 8 sts, 2 sc in next st; repeat from * around.

Round 20: Repeat Round 4—90 Puffs.

Round 21: Ch 1, sc in same st, sc in next 8 sts, 2 sc in next st, * sc in next 9 sts, 2 sc in next st; from * around.

Round 22: Repeat Round 4—99 Puffs.

Round 23: Ch 1, sc in same st, sc in next 9 sts, 2 sc in next st, * sc in next 10 sts, 2 sc in next st; repeat from * around.

Round 24: Repeat Round 4—108 Puffs.

Round 25: Ch 1, sc in same st, sc in next 10 sts, 2 sc in next st, * sc in next 11 sts, 2 sc in next st; repeat from * around—234 sts.

Round 26: Repeat Round 4—117 Puffs.

Round 27: Ch 1, sc in same st, sc in next 11 sts, 2 sc in next st, * sc in next 12 sts, 2 sc in next st; repeat from * around. Fasten off.

Finishing

Weave in ends.

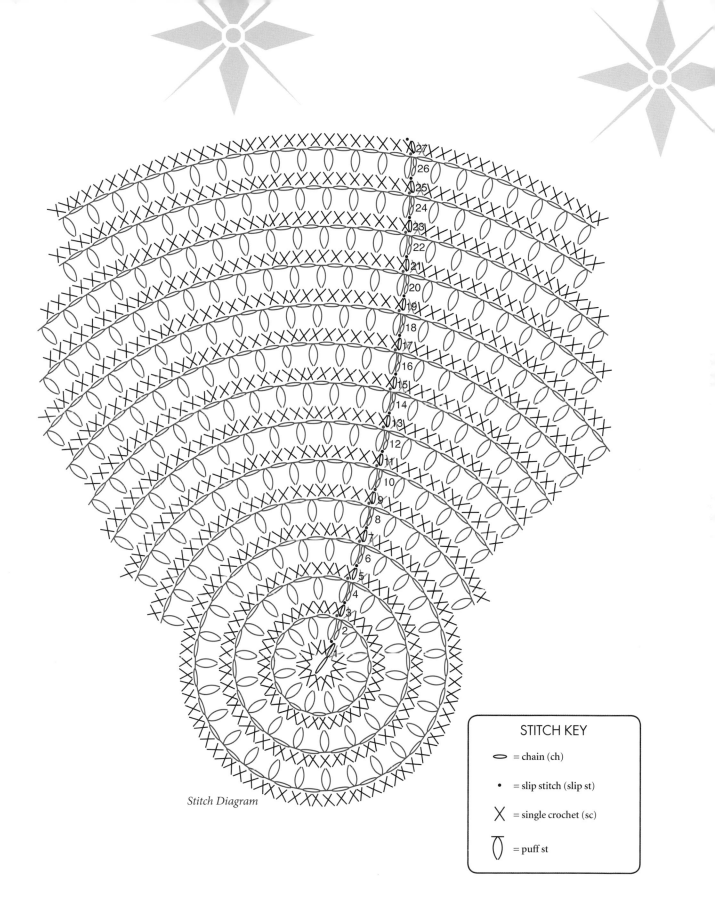

Stitch Diagram

STITCH KEY

⬯ = chain (ch)

• = slip stitch (slip st)

✕ = single crochet (sc)

⬯ = puff st

Elegant Pillow Case Edging

Have a housewarming or wedding shower coming up? Add your personal touch to the edge of pillow cases and sheets for an especially elegant and appreciated personal gift. Some things just don't change from decade to decade.

Adapted by Nazanin Fard

SIZES: *One size*

FINISHED MEASUREMENTS: *40"(102cm) long*

THREAD:

1 ball Aunt Lydia's® Classic Crochet Thread, size 10 (mercerized cotton, 350 yds [320m] per 2 oz ball) in color #210 Antique White

HOOK: *Size 7 (1.65mm) steel crochet hook*

NOTIONS: *Sewing needle and matching thread*

GAUGE: *9 dc = 1" (3cm)*

SPECIAL STITCHS:

Sc-Shell: (Sc, dc, ch 3, dc, sc) in next space

V-stitch: (Dc, ch 3, dc) in next space

Pattern Stitch:

Row 1 (RS): Dc in 4th ch from hook, dc in every ch across. Turn.

Row 2: Ch 3, 3 dc in same space, * 3 dc in next dc (block made), skip next 3 dc, sc in next dc, ch 3, 3 dc in same dc; repeat from * to end. Turn.

Row 3: Ch 1, * Sc-Shell in next ch-3 space, Sc-Shell in 2nd dc of next block; repeat from * to end. Turn.

Row 4: Ch 1, slip st in next 2 sts, slip st in ch-3 space, ch 6, dc in same ch-3 space, * V-stitch in next ch-3 space; repeat from * to end. Turn.

Row 5: Ch 1, * (sc, ch 3, sc) in next ch-3 space, (sc, ch 3, sc) in next dc; repeat from * to end.

Edging

Ch 376. Work Rows 1-5 of pattern st. Fasten off.

Finishing

Weave in ends. Block. Sew along edge of pillow case.

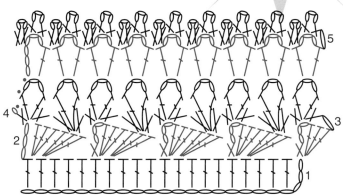

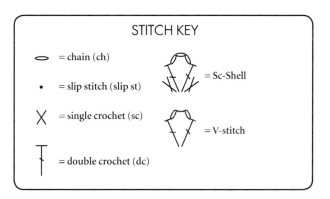

Stitch Diagram

STITCH KEY

= chain (ch)	
= slip stitch (slip st)	= Sc-Shell
X = single crochet (sc)	= V-stitch
T = double crochet (dc)	

Crochet Lacy Towel Edgings

There's no need to keep lace in the bedroom. A crocheted edging can turn a set of plain dish towels into charming nostalgic gifts. Ladies of the 1950s also embellished bed linens and even the edges of their cupboard shelves with crocheted lace.

Adapted by Sandy Harris

Edging 1

SIZES: *One size*

FINISHED MEASUREMENTS: *1"*
(3cm) wide × desired length

THREAD:
1 ball Aunt Lydia's® Classic Crochet Thread, size 10 (mercerized cotton, 300 yds [274.3 m] per 1.7 oz ball) in color #995 Ocean

HOOK: *Size 7 (1.65mm) steel crochet hook*

NOTIONS: *Sewing needle and matching thread*

GAUGE: *9 dc = 1" (3cm)*

Edging 2

SIZES: *One size*

FINISHED MEASUREMENTS: *⅞"*
(2cm) wide × desired length

THREAD:
1 ball Aunt Lydia's® Classic Crochet Thread, size 10 (mercerized cotton, 350 yds [320m] per 2 oz ball) in color #495 Wood Violet

HOOK: *Size 7 (1.65mm) steel crochet hook*

NOTIONS: *Sewing needle and matching thread*

GAUGE: *9 dc = 1" (3cm)*

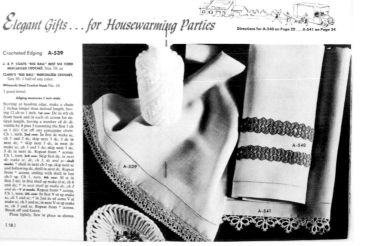

Crochet Lacy Towel Edging

Edging 1

Ch desired length for edging, making certain to have a multiple of 8 + 3.

Row 1: Dc in 4th ch from hook, dc in each ch across—multiple of 8 dc. Ch 6, turn.

Row 2: Dc in first dc, * skip next 3 dc, (2 dc, ch 3, 2 dc) in next dc, skip next 3 dc, (dc, ch 3, dc) in next dc; repeat from * across to last 4 dc (counting the starting ch at end of row as 1 dc), skip last 3 dc, in top of ch-3 work (dc, ch 3, dc). Ch 1, turn.

Row 3: Sc in next ch-3 space, * ch 7, sc in next ch-3 space; repeat from * across, ending with ch 7, sc in turning ch-6. Ch 1, turn.

Row 4: Sc in first sc, * in ch-7 loop work [ch 3, sc] 3 times, ch 3, sc in next sc; repeat from * across. Fasten off.

Finishing

Weave in ends. Press lightly, sew onto towel edge.

STITCH KEY

⬯	= chain (ch)	T	= double crochet (dc)
•	= slip stitch (slip st)		
X	= single crochet (sc)	⌢	= worked in back loop only
		⌣	= worked in front loop only

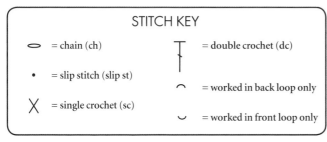

Edging 1 Stitch Diagram

Edging 2

Ch desired length for edging, making certain to have a multiple of 8 + 2.

Row 1: Sc in 2nd ch from hook and in each ch across—multiple of 8 + 1 sc. Ch 1, turn.

Row 2: Working in front loops only throughout, sc in first 4 sc, * (sc, ch 8, sc) in next sc, sc in next 7 sc; repeat from * across to last 5 sc, (sc, ch 8, sc) in next sc, sc in last 4 sc. Ch 3, turn.

Row 3: Working in back loops only throughout, skip first sc, sc in next sc, * skip next 3 sc, 9 sc in next loop, skip next 3 sc, sc in next sc, dc in next sc, sc in next sc; repeat from * across, ending with skip next 3 sc, 9 sc in next loop, skip next 3 sc, sc in next sc, dc in last sc. Ch 1, turn.

Row 4: Sc in first dc, * ch 4, sc in center sc of next loop, ch 5, sc in next sc, ch 4, sc in next dc; repeat from * across, working last sc on top of ch-3 instead of dc. Ch 1, turn.

Row 5 : Sc in first sc, * 3 sc in next ch-4 space, 5 sc in next ch-5 loop, 3 sc in next ch-4 space, sc in next sc; repeat from * across. Fasten off.

Finishing

Weave in ends. Press lightly, sew onto towel edge.

Edging 2 Stitch Diagram

Water Lily Appliqués

Add a bit of nostalgia to your bath with these cool, kitschy florals on plain inexpensive towels. These untraditional colors look great with today's neutral bathroom tiles.

Adapted by
Sandy Harris

SIZES: *One size*

FINISHED MEASUREMENTS:

LARGE FLOWER: *8½" (22cm) across, assembled*

SMALL FLOWER: *7" (18cm) across, assembled*

THREAD:

1 ball Aunt Lydia's® Classic Crochet Thread, size 10 (mercerized cotton, 350 yds [320m] per 2.3 oz ball) in each of colors #493 French Rose (A), #422 Golden Yellow (B), #310 Copper Mist (C)

HOOK: *Size 7 (1.65mm) steel crochet hook*

NOTIONS:

Sewing needle and matching thread
Washcloth or towel

GAUGE: *Gauge is not essential for this project.*

CLARK'S O.N.T. · J.&P. COATS   BATHROOM BEAUTIES   BOOK No. 265

Bathroom Beauties

DECORATIVE CROCHET FOR BATH TOWELS GUEST TOWELS FACE CLOTHS

10¢

Water Lily Appliqués

Large Flower

Large Petal

Make 6.

With A, ch 15.

Row 1 (RS): Sc in 2nd ch from hook, sc in next ch, hdc in next ch, dc in next ch, tr in next 6 ch, dc in next ch, hdc in next ch, sc in next 2 ch.

Now work in rounds as follows.

Round 1: Ch 3, sc in same place as last sc, working along opposite side of starting ch, sc in each ch across, ch 3, sc in each st across, ending with slip st in ch-3 space.

Round 2: Ch 3, 4 dc in same space, dc in each sc around, working 5 dc in ch-3 space, slip st in top of ch-3.

Round 3: Sc in same place as slip st, sc in next dc, in next dc work (sc, ch 3, sc), sc in each dc until center dc of next 5-dc group, then (sc, ch 3, sc) in this st; sc in each dc around. Join and fasten off.

Small Petal

Make 4.

With A, work as for large petal through Round 1. Fasten off.

Stamen

Make 1.

With B, ch 10.

First Spoke: Yo, insert hook in 3rd ch from hook, draw loop through, [yo, insert hook in same ch, draw loop through] twice, yo and draw through all loops on hook (Clones Knot made), slip st in next ch and each ch across.

Second Spoke: Ch 10, work as for First Spoke, ending with slip st in same place as last slip st on First Spoke. Make 5 more spokes, ending each one same as Second Spoke. Fasten off.

Bud

Make 4.

With A, work as for Large Petal through Round 1.

Round 2: 3 sc in same space as slip st, sc in each sc around to next space, sc in space, ch 4, sc in 4th ch from hook (picot made), 2 sc in same space, sc in each remaining sc around. Join and fasten off.

Stem

Make 4.

With C, ch 20.

Row 1: Sc in second ch from hook and in each ch across. Fasten off.

Large Leaf

Make 2.

With C, ch 15.

Row 1 (right side): Sc in second ch from hook, hdc in next ch, dc in next ch, tr in next 9 ch, dc in next ch, 5 hdc in next ch; working along opposite side of starting chain, dc in next ch, tr in next 9 ch, dc in next ch, hdc in next ch, sc in next ch. Ch 3, turn.

Row 2: Skip first sc, dc2tog over next 2 sts, [2 dc in next st, dc in next st] 5 times, 2 dc in each of the next 5 sts, [dc in next st, 2 dc in next st] 5 times, dc2tog, dc. Ch 3, turn.

Row 3: Skip first dc, dc2tog, dc in next dc, [2 dc in next dc, dc in next 2 dc] 5 times, 2 dc in each of next 6 dc, [dc in next 2 dc, 2 dc in next dc] 5 times,

dc in next dc, dc2tog, dc in top of turning ch. Ch 3, turn.

Row 4: Skip first dc, dc2tog, * dc in next 3 dc, 2 dc in next dc; repeat from * around to last 3 sts, dc2tog, dc in top of turning ch. Ch 1, turn.

Row 5: Skip first dc, sc in next dc, hdc in next dc, dc2tog, dc in next 2 dc, * 2 dc in next dc, dc in next 3 dc; repeat from * to last 5 sts, dc2tog, hdc in next dc, sc in next dc, slip st in last st. Ch 1, do not turn.

To complete: Work sc across end of leaf to center, slip st, ch 7, slip st in 2nd ch from hook and each ch across, slip st in same place on leaf, sc around rest of leaf. Fasten off.

Small Leaf

Make 2.

Work as for Large Leaf through Row 3.

Row 4: Working across top, complete as for Large Leaf. Fasten off.

Small Flower

Make all as for Large Flower.

Small Petals: Make 10.

Stamen: Make 1.

Buds: Make 2.

Stems: Make 2.

Small Leaves: Make 2.

Finishing

Sew Large and Small Petals together to form Water Lily, sew Stamen to center. Sew Water Lily to towel or washcloth along with Leaves, Stems and Buds as shown. Weave in ends.

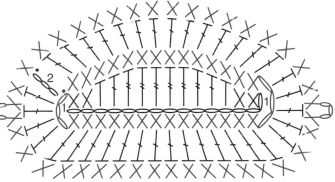

Large Leaf Stitch Diagram

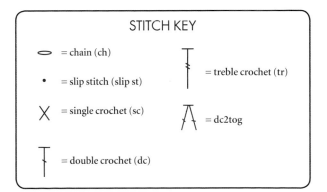

Large Petal Stitch Diagram

STITCH KEY	
⬯ = chain (ch)	┬ = treble crochet (tr)
• = slip stitch (slip st)	
✕ = single crochet (sc)	⋀ = dc2tog
┬ = double crochet (dc)	

Spice Rug

Bet you never thought of crocheting a rug for your bedroom or bathroom! This one is done in squares. So if the size doesn't suit your space, you can add or subtract squares. Make it in easy-care yarn and toss it in the washer and dryer.

Adapted by Tammy Hebert

SIZES: *One size*

FINISHED MEASUREMENTS: *42"*
   × 28" (107cm × 71cm)

YARN:

*10 skeins Red Heart® Eco-Ways®
   (acrylic/recycled polyester, 186 yds
   [170m] per 4 oz skein) in color
   #3422 Yam*

HOOK: *Size I (5.5mm) crochet hook*

NOTIONS: *Yarn needle*

GAUGE: *12 sts and 12 rows = 4"*
   (10cm)

NOTE: Use 2 strands of yarn held together throughout.

Rug

Block

Make 6.

With 2 strands held double, ch 28.

Row 1 (WS): Sc in 2nd ch from hook and in each ch across—27 sc. Ch 1, turn.

Row 2: Sc in each sc across. Ch 1, turn. Repeat Row 2 until 26 rows have been completed. Do not cut yarn.

Round 1 (RS): 3 sc in side of last sc, sc in end of next 25 rows, 3 sc in corner, sc in beginning ch

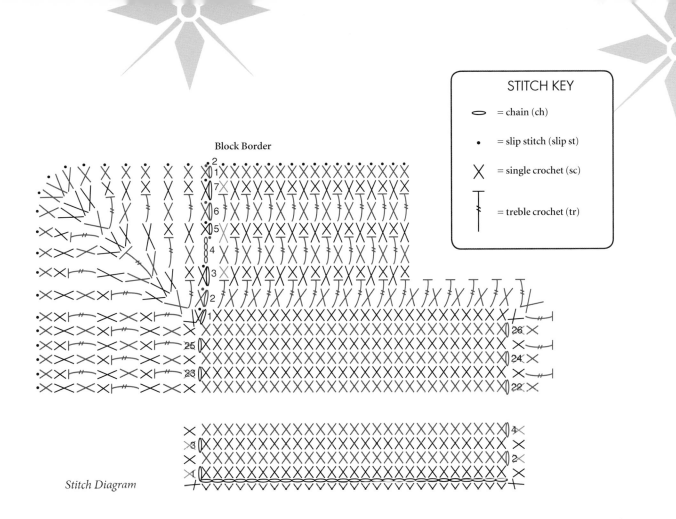

Block Border

Stitch Diagram

across, 3 sc in corner, sc in end of 25 rows, 3 sc in corner, sc in each sc across; join with slip st in first sc of corner 3-sc group.

Round 2: Ch 1, sc in same place as slip st, * in center sc of 3-sc group work tr, sc, tr, [sc in next sc, tr in next sc] 13 times, sc in next sc; repeat from * around. Join.

Round 3: Ch 1, sc in same place as slip st and in each st around, working 3 sc in center st of each corner. Join.

Round 4: Ch 4, sc in next sc, tr in next sc, * in center sc of corner work sc, tr, sc, [tr in next sc, sc in next sc] 15 times, tr in next sc; repeat from * 2 times, in center sc of corner work sc, tr, sc, [tr in next sc, sc in next sc] 14 times, tr in next sc. Join.

Round 5: Repeat Round 3.

Round 6: Ch 1, sc in same place as slip st, [tr in next sc, sc in next sc] twice, * in center sc of next

corner work tr, sc, tr, [sc in next sc, tr in next sc] 17 times, sc in next sc; repeat from * 2 times, in center sc of corner work tr, sc, tr, [sc in next sc, tr in next sc] 15 times, sc in next sc. Join.

Round 7: Repeat Round 3. Join and weave in ends.

Finishing

Sew 2 rows of 3 squares neatly together.

Border

Round 1 (RS): Attach a double strand of yarn to any corner, * 3 sc in corner sc, sc in each sc across; repeat from * 3 times.

Round 2: Slip st in each sc around. Join and weave in ends.

Block to measurements.

69

Simplicity in Stripes Rug

Whoever the clever lady was who thought of this technique has our admiration. She made her rug extra thick and sturdy by crocheting over ten long strands of yarn. Our multi-colored yarn version will help hide the dirt.

*Adapted by
Kim Kotary*

SIZES: *One size*

FINISHED SIZE: *Measures: 38″ × 23½″ (97cm × 60cm)*

YARN:

3 skeins Red Heart® Super Saver® (acrylic, 364 yds [333m] per 7 oz skein) in color #360 Café (A)

3 skeins Red Heart® Super Saver® Prints (acrylic, 244 yds [233m] per 5 oz skein) in color #947 Marrakesh (B)

HOOK: *Size I (5.5mm) crochet hook*

NOTIONS: *Yarn needle*

GAUGE: *14 sc and 7 rows = 4″ (10cm)*

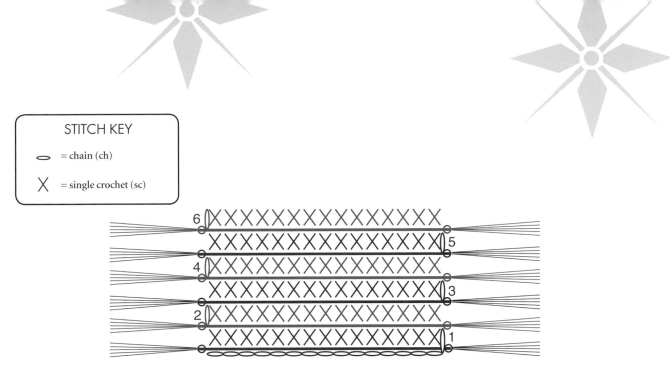

STITCH KEY

⬭ = chain (ch)

X = single crochet (sc)

Stitch Diagram

Bundles

Make 23 with A and 22 with B.

Cut 10 strands, each 45" (114cm) long. Knot all strands together 3" (8cm) in from each end using an overhand knot. Knots should be secure but not too tight; they may need adjusting later.

Rug

With A, ch 111.

Row 1: Hold 1 bundle of A on top of ch and, working between the knots, sc over the bundle and in the 2nd ch from hook and each ch across. Fasten off, leaving a 3" (8cm) tail—110 sc.

Row 2: With B, leaving a 3" (8cm) tail and starting with a slip knot on the hook, sc over a bundle of B and in each sc across. Fasten off leaving a 3" (8cm) tail.

Row 3: With A, leaving a 3" (8cm) tail and starting with a slip knot on the hook, sc over a bundle of A and in each sc across. Fasten off leaving a 3" (8cm) tail.

Repeat Rows 2 and 3 until all bundles are used.

Finishing

With yarn needle, pull tails through the knots on each end. Adjust bundles, stitch spacing and knots as necessary. Trim fringe evenly.

All the comforts of Home . . . . WITH THE EXTRA ATTRACTION OF A COZY AFGHAN

Chapter Four

Cozy Rooms

Crocheted afghans make a room seem more inviting and are practical for staying cozy. Have fun choosing a design to complement each chair, sofa and bed in your home and then make a few for gifting. You'll find four pillows in this chapter, too.

Tally-Ho Afghan & Pillow

You may not see the appeal of decorating a great room or study with pictures of hunters, but you'll love this afghan pattern. It's amazing how a new pattern emerges when you use three yarn colors.

Adapted by Beth Bishop

SIZES: *One size*

FINISHED MEASUREMENTS:

AFGHAN: *46" × 57" (117cm × 145cm)*

PILLOW: *16" (41cm) square*

YARN:

1 skein Red Heart® Super Saver® (acrylic, 364 yds [333m] per 7 oz skein) in color #320 Cornmeal (A)

4 skeins Red Heart® Super Saver® (acrylic, 364 yds [333m] per 7 oz skein) in color #336 Warm Brown (B)

5 skeins Red Heart® Super Saver® Prints (acrylic, 244 yds [233m] per 5 oz skein) in color #931 Seagrass (C)

HOOK: *Size J (6mm) crochet hook*

NOTIONS:

Yarn needle

16" (41cm) pillow form

GAUGE: *Motif = 5½" (14cm) square*

Tally-Ho No. 6140 . . . Directions on Page 10

·9·

Tally-Ho Afghan & Pillow

Motif

Make 80 for afghan; make 18 for pillow. Starting at center with A, ch 4. Join with slip st to form a ring.

Round 1: Ch 3, 2 dc in ring, [ch 1, 3 dc in ring] 3 times, ch 1, insert hook in 3rd ch of ch-3, join B and make a slip st. Fasten off A.

Round 2: With B, ch 1, work sc in same place as slip st, sc in next 2 dc, [5 sc in next ch-1 space (corner made), sc in next 3 dc] 3 times, 5 sc in last ch-1 space. Join, drop B.

Round 3: Join C, ch 3, * dc in each sc to center sc of corner, leaving the last 2 loops of last dc on hook, drop C, draw B through 2 loops on hook, 5 dc in B in corner sc, leaving last 2 loops of last dc on hook, change to C; repeat from * around, ending with 2 "C" dc. Join.

Round 4: Ch 3, * dc in each "C" dc, change to B as before and dc in next 3 dc, change to C and make 3 dc in same place as last dc, change to B and make another dc in same place as last dc, dc in next 2 dc, change to C; repeat from * around. Join and fasten off.

Afghan

Arrange in 8 rows of 10 blocks and sew together neatly on WS using B.

Finishing

Border:

Round 1: Join B to one corner, ch 1, * 3 sc in corner, sc in each dc to next corner; repeat from * around, join.

Rounds 2-5: Ch 1, sc in each sc, working 3 sc in center sc of each corner and working Round 4 with A. Join. Fasten off at end of 5th round.

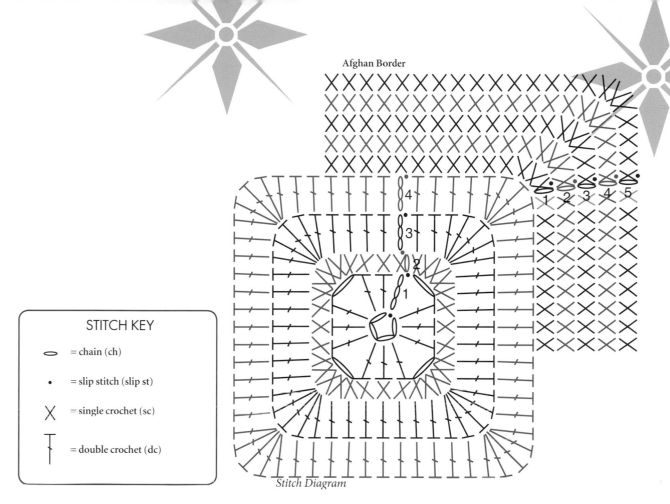

Afghan Border

STITCH KEY

◯ = chain (ch)

• = slip stitch (slip st)

✕ = single crochet (sc)

┬ = double crochet (dc)

Stitch Diagram

Pillow

Arrange in 3 rows of 3 blocks and sew together neatly on WS using B. Make 2nd piece same as first.

Finishing

Round 1: With WS together, join B to one corner, working through both loops of front and back pieces, ch 1, * 3 sc in corner, sc in each dc to next corner; repeat from * around next two sides, insert pillow form, and continue along last side as established. Join.
Round 2: With A, ch 1, sc in each sc, working 3 sc in center sc of each corner. Join.
Round 3: With B, repeat Round 2. Join. Fasten off.

Lazy Daisy Afghan

Once you spot the one hexagon-shape motif, you'll understand how this fascinating throw is put together. Our vibrant golden color combination will give anyone a brighter outlook. It would also be wonderful in softer pastels or muted neutrals.

Adapted by
Bobbi Anderson

SIZES: *One size*

FINISHED MEASUREMENTS:
   44″ × 63″ (112cm × 160cm), excluding border

YARN:

5 skeins Red Heart® Super Saver® (acrylic, 364 yds [333m] per 7 oz skein) in color #320 Cornmeal (A)

3 skeins Red Heart® Super Saver® (acrylic, 364 yds [333m] per 7 oz skein) in color #624 Tea Leaf (B)

1 skeins Red Heart® Super Saver® (acrylic, 364 yds [333m] per 7 oz skein) in color #256 Carrot (C)

HOOK: *Size I (5.5mm) crochet hook*

NOTIONS: *Yarn needle*

GAUGE: *Motif = 7½″ (19cm) across, point to point*

SPECIAL ABBREVIATIONS:

Beginning pc (popcorn): Ch 3 (counts as dc), 3 dc in same st, remove hook from loop and insert from front to back into top of beginning ch-3 and into dropped loop, pull dropped loop through, pull to tighten and push pc to front of work, ch 1.

Pc (popcorn): Work four dc in indicated st, remove hook from loop and insert from front to back into top of first dc and into dropped loop, pull dropped loop through, pull to tighten and push pc to front of work, ch 1.

Dec dc (decrease double crochet): [Yo, insert hook in next st or space, pull loop through, yo and pull through 2 loops on hook] twice, yo, pull through remaining 3 loops on hook.

NOTE: *Whenever possible, work over tails to save time and have fewer ends to weave in.*

SPECIAL TECHNIQUE:

Adjustable ring: Wrap yarn around your finger leaving a 6″ (15cm) end. Insert hook into the wrap and draw up a loop; ch 1 to secure loop and then remove from finger. Work stitches of Round 1 into the ring. Pull end to tighten ring.

Lazy Daisy Afghan

Afghan

Motif

Make 60.

Round 1: With A, using adjustable ring method, work 12 sc in ring, join with slip st to first sc; OR, ch 2, work 12 sc in second ch from hook, join with slip st to first sc. Fasten off—12 sc.

Round 2: Join B to any sc, beginning pc in first sc, pc in each sc around, join with slip st to first pc. Fasten off, tighten ring—12 pc.

Round 3: Join A to any space between pc, 2 sc in same space, 2 sc in next space, ch 3, * [2 sc in next space] twice, ch 3; repeat from * around, join with slip st to first sc. Fasten off—24 sc, 6 ch-3 spaces.

Round 4: Join C in same space as slip st. Ch 3 (counts as dc), dc in next 3 sts, in next ch-3 space work (2 dc, ch 1, 2 dc), * dc in next 4 sts, in next ch-3 space work (2 dc, ch 1, 2 dc); repeat from * around, join with slip st in first dc. Fasten off.

Note: Read through following instructions before proceeding. You will be changing color from B to C and back to B. See photo.

Chg dc (color change dc):
With old color (B or C), work dc in indicated st until 2 loops remain on hook, yo with new color (B or C) and pull through remaining 2 loops on hook, color change made. Do not fasten off; carry unused color, working over it.

Round 5: Join B in any ch-1 space, ch 4 (counts as dc and ch-1), chg dc in same space, chg dc in next dc, dc in next 5 dc, [chg dc in next dc] twice, *(dc, ch 1, chg dc) in next space, chg dc in next dc, dc in next 5 dc, [chg dc in next dc] twice; repeat from *

around, join to 3rd ch of beginning ch-4 as follows: insert hook in ch, lay C over hook to bring it up to next row, with B complete slip st.

Round 6: With B, slip st in next space, ch 4 (counts as dc and ch-1), dc in same space, [chg dc in next dc] twice, dc in next 5 dc, [chg dc in next dc] twice, * dc in next dc, (dc, ch 1, dc) in next space, [chg dc in next dc] twice, dc in next 5 dc, [chg dc in next dc] twice; repeat from * around, end with dc in slip st from Round 5, join with slip st in 3rd ch of beginning ch-4. Fasten off B and C.

Stitch Diagram

STITCH KEY

⬭ = chain (ch)

• = slip stitch (slip st)

X = single crochet (sc)

T = double crochet (dc)

🮑 = beginning popcorn (beginning pc)

🮑 = popcorn (pc)

Finishing

With B, sew motifs together making 4 strips of 9 motifs and 3 strips of 8 motifs. Referring to chart for placement, sew strips together.

Border

With RS facing, join C to any stitch, dc in each st around working (dc, ch 1, dc) in each ch-1 space at outer points, and work dec dc at each inner point. Join with slip st in beginning dc. Fasten off. Weave in ends.

Assembly Diagram

Trophy Afghan

Whoever first designed this classic crocheted ripple is a gold trophy winner in our books! Unfortunately, records of the designer are long gone. We show our Trophy Afghan made with three shades, but this is a design that looks wonderful no matter how many colors you use.

Adapted by
Marianne Forrestal

SIZES: *One size*

FINISHED MEASURMENT: *45" × 55" (114cm × 140cm)*

YARN:

2 skeins Red Heart® Super Saver® (acrylic, 364 yds [333m] per 7 oz skein) in each of colors #406 Medium Thyme (A), #378 Claret (C)

3 skeins Red Heart® Super Saver® Prints (acrylic, 244 yds [233m] per 5 oz skein) in color #944 Cherry Cola (B)

HOOK: *Size K (6.5mm) crochet hook*

NOTIONS: *Yarn needle*

GAUGE: *7½" (19cm) between peaks of ripples; 8 rows = 4" (10cm) in pattern*

COLOR SEQUENCE: *8 rows A, 4 rows B, 8 rows C, 10 rows B, 8 rows C, 4 rows B, 8 rows A, 10 rows B, 8 rows A, 4 rows B, 8 rows C, 10 rows B, 8 rows C, 4 rows B, 8 rows A*

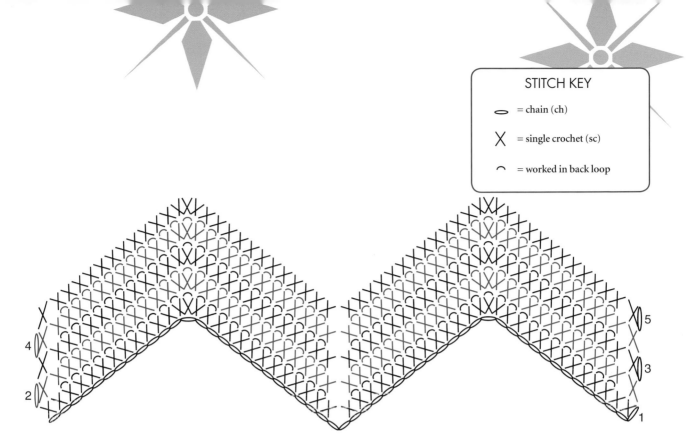

Stitch Diagram

Afghan

With A, ch 161.

Row 1 (RS): Sc in 2nd ch from hook, sc in next 11 ch, [3 sc in next ch, sc in next 12 ch, skip next 2 ch, sc in next 12 ch] 5 times, 3 sc in next ch, sc in last 12 ch, ch 1, turn.

Note: Except for first and last sc of each row, all sts are worked in the back loop only from now on.

Row 2: Sc in both loops of first st, skip next st, sc in next 11 sts, [3 sc in next st, sc in next 12 sts, skip next 2 sts, sc in next 12 sts] 5 times, 3 sc in next st, sc in next 11 sts, skip next st, sc in both loops of last st, ch 1, turn.

Rows 3–110: Repeat Row 2, following color sequence on page 82.

Finishing

Weave in ends.

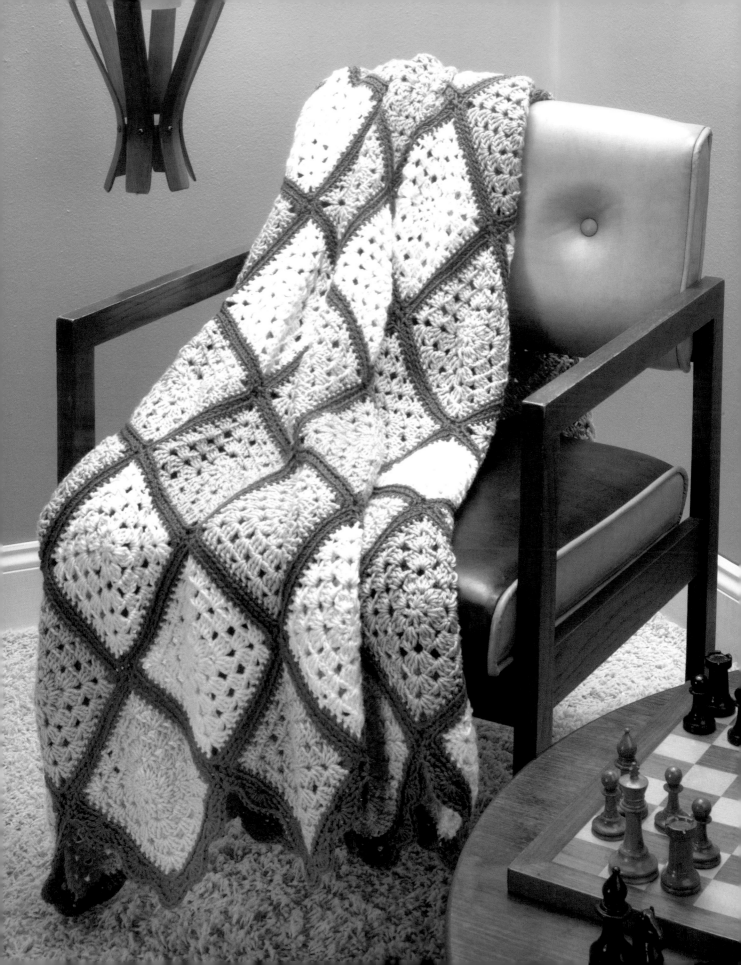

Carnival Granny Afghan

This updated version of a traditional granny afghan is easy to crochet and can be adapted to any room or color scheme. One thing about that "good ol' granny," she is never boring. Take granny squares along and keep your hands out of trouble wherever life may lead you.

Adapted by
Marianne Forrestal

SIZES: *One size*

FINISHED MEASUREMENTS:
55″ × 66″ (140cm × 168cm)

YARN:

3 skeins Red Heart® Eco-Ways® (acrylic/recycled polyester, 186 yds [170m] per 4 oz skein) in each of colors #3313 Oyster (A), #1615 Lichen (C)

4 skeins Red Heart® Eco-Ways® (acrylic/recycled polyester, 186 yds [170m] per 4 oz skein) in each of colors #3114 Chamois (B), #3518 Peacock (D)

HOOK: *Size H (5mm) crochet hook*

NOTIONS: *Yarn needle*

GAUGE: *Rounds 1-5 = 6″ (15cm)*

SPECIAL ABBREVIATIONS:

BC (beginning cluster): Ch 2, [yo, insert hook in same st as ch 2, yo and pull up a loop, yo and pull through 1 loop on hook, yo and pull through 2 loops on hook] twice, yo and pull through all 3 loops on hook.

Cluster: Yo, insert hook in st, yo and pull up a loop, yo and pull through 1 loop on hook, yo and pull through 2 loops on hook, [yo, insert hook in same st, yo and pull up a loop, yo and pull through 1 loop on hook, yo and pull through 2 loops on hook] twice, yo and pull through all 4 loops on hook.

sc3tog: [Insert hook in next st, yo, draw yarn through st] 3 times, yo, draw yarn through all 4 loops on hook.

Afghan

Square

Make 23 each in A and C, 26 in B—72 total.

Ch 4, slip st in first ch to form ring.

Round 1: Ch 4, [dc in ring, ch 1] 7 times, join with slip st to 3rd ch of starting ch-4.

Round 2: Slip st in first ch-1 space, BC in same space, ch 3, [cluster, ch 3 in next ch-1 space] 7 times, join with slip st in top of BC.

Round 3: Slip st in first ch-3 space, ch 3, 2 dc in same space, ch 1, *(3 dc, ch 2, 3 dc) in next ch-3

Carnival Granny Afghan

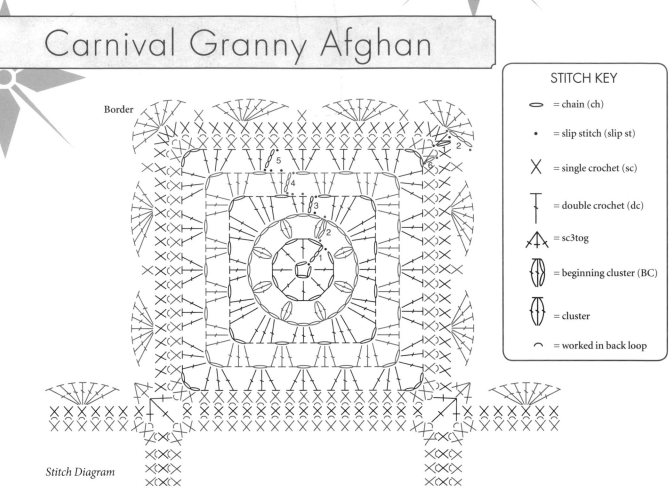

Border

Stitch Diagram

space, ch 1, 3 dc, ch 1 in next ch-3 space; repeat from * twice more, (3 dc, ch 2, 3 dc) in next ch-3 space, ch 1, join with slip st in top of starting ch-3.

Round 4: Slip st in next 2 dc and ch-1 space, ch 3, 2 dc in same space, ch 1, *(3 dc, ch 2, 3 dc) in next ch-2 space, ch 1, [3 dc, ch 1 in next ch-1 space] twice; repeat from * twice more, (3 dc, ch 2, 3 dc) in next ch-2 space, ch 1, (3 dc, ch 1) in next ch-1 space, join with slip st in top of starting ch-3.

Round 5: Slip st in next 2 dc and ch-1 space, ch 3, 2 dc in same space, *(3 dc, ch 3, 3 dc) in next ch-2 space, [3 dc in next ch-1 space] 3 times; repeat from * twice more, (3 dc, ch 3, 3 dc) in next ch-2 space, [3 dc in next ch-1 space] twice, join with slip st in top of starting ch-3. Fasten off.

Round 6: Join D with slip st in any ch-3 corner space, ch 1, 3 sc in same space, sc in each dc (15 on each side) and 3 sc in each ch-3 corner space around, join with slip st to first sc. Fasten off D. Weave in ends.

Finishing

With D, hold 2 squares together with RS facing, and join with sc in back loops only. This will leave the "ridge" created by the sc on the WS and RS flat with front loops of squares showing. Following the diagram for color placement on page 87, make two rows each of 3, 5, 7 ,9 and 11 squares, plus 2 single squares. Again following diagram for row placement, sc rows together in same manner as joining squares.

Border

Round 1: Working entire round in back loops only, with RS facing, join D with slip st in back loop of center sc of highest corner of top left square (square is in C), ch 1, 3 sc in same st, sc in next 17 sts, 3 sc in next st, sc in next 17 sts, sc next 3 sts tog in following manner: insert hook in next st, yo and draw up a loop, insert hook in corner st of square one row below (B square), yo and draw up a loop, insert hook in first st of next square (B square), yo and draw up a loop, yo and draw through all 3 loops on hook. Each inside corner is done the same way. [Sc in next 17 sts, 3 sc in next st, sc in next 17 sts, sc next 3 sts tog] 5 times, sc in next 17 sts, 3 sc in next st, [sc in next 17 sts, 3 sc in next st, sc in next 17 sts, sc next 3 sts tog] 5 times, sc in

Assembly Diagram

next 17 sts, 3 sc in next st, [sc in next 17 sts, 3 sc in next st, sc in next 17 sts, sc next 3 sts tog] 6 times, sc in next 17 sts, 3 sc in next st, [sc in next 17 sts, 3 sc in next st, sc in next 17 sts, sc next 3 sts tog] 5 times, sc in next 17 sts, join with slip st to first sc.

Round 2: Working this round in both loops, slip st in next sc, ch 3, 6 dc in same sc, **skip next 2 sc, sc in next sc, skip next 2 sc, 7 dc in next sc, skip next 3 sc, sc in next sc, skip next 3 sc, 7 dc in next sc, skip next 2 sc, sc in next sc, skip next 2 sc, 7 dc in next (corner) sc**, *skip next 2 sc, sc in next sc, skip next 2 sc, 7 dc in next sc, skip next 3 sc, sc in next sc, skip next 3 sc, 7 dc in next sc, skip next 3 sc, sc next 3 st tog, skip next 3 sc, 7 dc in next sc, skip next 3 sc, sc in next sc, skip next 2 sc, 7 dc in next sc, skip next 2 sc, sc in next sc, skip next 2 sc, 7 dc in next (corner) sc*, repeat between *'s 5 times more, repeat between **'s once, repeat between *'s 5 times, repeat between **'s once, repeat between *'s 6 times, repeat between **'s once, repeat between *'s 4 times, skip next 2 sc, sc in next sc, skip next 2 sc, 7 dc in next sc, skip next 2 sc, sc in next sc, skip next 3 sc, 7 dc in next sc, skip next 3 sc, sc next 3 sc tog, skip next 3 sc, 7 dc in next sc, skip next 3 sc, sc in next sc, skip next 2 sc, 7 dc in next sc, skip next 2 sc, sc in next sc, skip next 2 sc, join with slip st to top of starting ch-3. Fasten off. Weave in ends.

Caprice Afghan

This original may have been designed over 50 years ago, but the new Caprice couldn't look more up-to-date. You'll love the way the edges of the squares come together and form an X. This graphic design will keep you cozy anywhere you choose.

Adapted by
Beth Bishop

SIZES: *One size*

FINISHED MEASUREMENTS:
  48" × 64" (122cm × 163cm)

YARN:

5 skeins Red Heart® Soft Yarn (acrylic, 256 yds [234m] per 5 oz skein) in each of colors #9522 Leaf (A) and #3720 Lavender (B)

2 skeins Red Heart® Soft Yarn (acrylic, 256 yds [234m] per 5 oz skein) in color #3729 Grape (C)

HOOK: *Size J (6mm) crochet hook*

NOTIONS: *Yarn needle*

GAUGE: *1 motif = 5¾" (15cm) square*

Afghan

Motif

Make 32.

With C and starting at center, ch 4, join with slip st to form a ring.

Round 1: Ch 3 (counts as dc), work 2 dc, ch 2, 3 dc, ch 2, 3 dc, ch 2, 3 dc, ch 2 in ring, join with slip st in 3rd st of starting ch-3.

Round 2: Ch 2, yo, insert hook in top of beginning ch-3 and draw up a loop, yo, insert hook in next dc and draw up a loop, yo and draw through all loops on hook, ch 1 tightly (cluster made). Yo, insert hook in same dc and draw up a loop, yo, insert hook in next dc and draw up a loop, complete cluster as before, *work cluster in first ch of corner ch-2, ch 2, work cluster in next ch**, work 2 clusters as before over next 3 dc; repeat from * around, ending last rep at **, join with slip st. Fasten off.

Round 3: Join A to 2nd ch of corner, ch 2, work cluster in same ch, insert hook in next cluster (not in ch-1) and draw up a loop, yo, insert hook in ch-1 of same cluster and draw up a loop, yo and draw through all loops, ch 1. Work cluster above each of next 3 clusters in same manner, cluster in first ch of corner, ch 2, cluster in next ch of corner; continue along second side, ending with cluster in first ch of corner. Join B and draw through loop on hook (creating a ch), (drop A to front of work), with B, ch 1, cluster in next ch of corner,

Caprice Afghan

work cluster above each of the next 4 clusters, cluster in first ch of corner, ch 2, cluster in next ch of corner; continue along last side ending with cluster in first ch of corner, ch 2, join with slip st—6 clusters on each side.

Round 4: Turn, (drop B to front of work), skip next ch, join A with slip st in next ch. With A, ch 2, turn, work cluster in corner ch, work cluster above each of next 6 clusters, cluster in first ch of corner ch, ch 2, cluster in next ch of corner; continue along second side, ending with cluster in first ch of corner. Draw B through loop on hook (creating a ch), (drop A to front of work), ch 1, cluster in next ch of corner, work cluster above each of next 6 clusters, cluster in first ch of corner ch, ch 2, cluster in next ch of corner; continue along last side, ending with cluster in first ch of corner, ch 2, join with slip st—8 clusters on each side.

Round 5: Repeat Round 4 with A and B, working over 8 clusters on each side, join with slip st. Fasten off—10 clusters on each side.

Finishing

Join blocks as shown in diagram on page 91, working seams from the WS. Finished afghan will be 5–6 blocks wide and 7–8 blocks long.

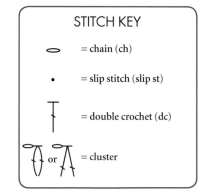

Stitch Diagram

STITCH KEY	
⬭	= chain (ch)
•	= slip stitch (slip st)
⊤	= double crochet (dc)
⬭ or 人	= cluster

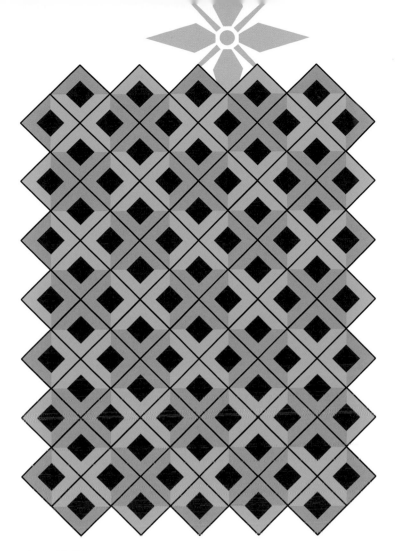

Assembly Diagram

Mardi Gras Afghan

The interpretation of this beauty looks more like a quiet evening at home with a good book than a New Orleans Mardi Gras parade (upper right in vintage image). Isn't it fun to see how the choice of colors can change the way you feel about an afghan?

Adapted by
Katherine Eng

SIZES: *One size*

FINISHED MEASUREMENTS:
   46" × 57" (117cm × 145cm)

YARN:

3 skeins Red Heart® Soft Yarn (acrylic, 256 yds [234m] per 5 oz skein) in color #9440 Light Grey Heather (A)

5 skeins Red Heart® Soft Yarn (acrylic, 256 yds [234m] per 5 oz skein) in each of colors #9518 Teal (B), #9388 Wheat (C)

HOOK: *Size H (5mm) crochet hook*

NOTIONS: *Yarn needle*

GAUGE: *Motif = 7¼" (18cm) square*

SPECIAL STITCH:
Shell: 5 dc in same space

NOTE: *Always join last st to first with a slip st.*

Mardi Gras Afghan

Afghan

Motif

Make 42.

With A, ch 6. Join in a ring. Ch 3 (counts as first dc of round throughout).

Round 1: Work 23 dc in ring, join—24 dc.

Round 2: Ch 5, dtr in same dc (top of ch-3), ch 5, slip st in same st (corner 1 made), * sc in next dc, skip next dc, shell in next dc, skip next dc, sc in next dc, (slip st, ch 5, dtr, ch 5, slip st) in next dc; repeat from * around. Join and fasten off.

With C, draw up a loop in any corner dtr and ch 1.

Round 3: Sc in same st, * (tr, 4 dc) in next sc, sc in back loop of center dc of next shell, (4 dc, tr) in next sc, sc in next corner dtr; repeat from * around, join to beginning sc, drop C. Draw a loop of B through loop on hook.

Note: On remaining rounds, hold dropped color behind sts being worked in new color. Then pick up the dropped yarn when specified and work over the alternate color. Always pull new color to front, dropping last color to back. At end of Rounds 4 and 5, untangle twisted yarn before proceeding.

Round 4: Ch 3, work 4 dc in same sc. Holding back on hook last 2 loops of last dc, drop B, pick up C and draw through 2 loops on hook (from here on, change color in this manner). * Working over unused color, dc in each st across to within sc of next corner, changing color on last dc, ** work 5 dc in corner sc, changing color on last dc; repeat from * around, ending at ** on last repeat. Join to top of ch-3—11 "C" dc between "B" sts on each side).

Round 5: Ch 3, dc in next dc, * 5 dc in center dc of corner, dc in next 3 dc, changing color on last dc, dc in each dc to within last "C" dc, changing color on last dc. Dc in last "C" dc ** and in next 2 dc;

repeat from * around, ending at ** on last repeat. Join to top of ch-3.

Round 6: Ch 3, dc in next 3 dc, * (dc, tr, ch 1, tr, dc) in center dc of corner, dc in next 6 dc, changing color on last dc. Dc in each dc to within last "C" dc, changing color on last dc, ** dc in next 6 dc; repeat from * around, ending at ** on last repeat. Dc in last 2 dc. Join and fasten off.

Finishing

Weave in ends. Sew motifs together in 6 strips of 7 squares each using a whipstitch. Sew strips together.

Border

With C and RS facing, draw up a loop in center dc of any motif, ch 1.

Round 1 (RS): Sc in each dc, tr and in each corner ch-1 space at joining seams, hdc in each joining seam and (sc, ch 2, sc) in each of 4 corner ch-1 spaces. Join. Ch 1, turn—155 sts each width and 181 sts each length.

Round 2: Sc in next sc, * ch 1, skip 1 sc, sc in next sc (or in next hdc); repeat from * around, working at each corner: ch 1, skip 1 sc, (sc, ch 2, sc) in corner ch-2 space. At end of round, join. Ch 1, turn.

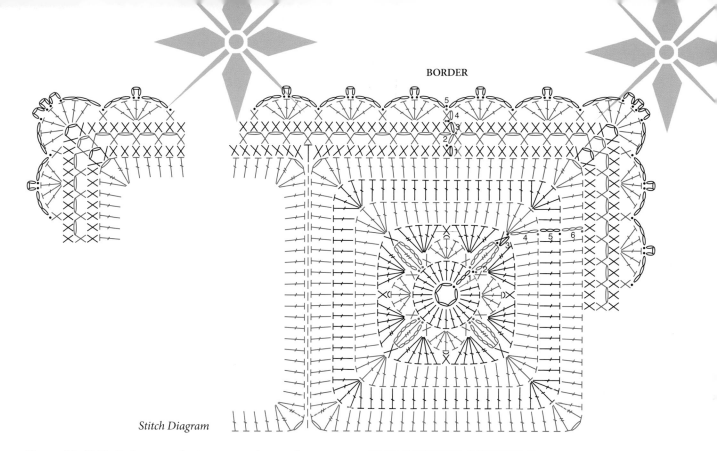

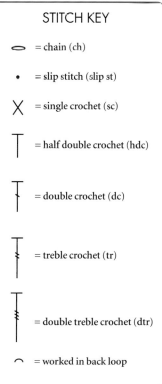

Stitch Diagram

Round 3 (RS): Sc in next ch-1 space and in each sc and remaining ch-1 space around, working (sc, ch 2, sc) in each corner ch-2 space. Join and fasten off. With B and RS facing, draw up a loop in 15th sc to the left of corner ch-2 space on either long side edge. Ch 1.

Round 4 (RS): Sc in same sc, * skip 2 sc, shell in next sc, skip 2 sc, sc in next sc; repeat from * around, working at corners 1 and 3: skip 2 sc, 7 dc in corner ch-2 space, skip 1 sc, sc in next sc. At corners 2 and 4: skip 1 sc, 7 dc in corner ch-2 space, skip 2 sc, sc in next sc. At end of round, skip last 2 sc, join last dc of last shell to beginning sc.

Round 5 (RS): * Ch 3, (slip st, ch 3, slip st) in center dc of next shell, ch 3, slip st in next sc; repeat from * around, working at each corner: ch 3, skip 2 dc, slip st in next dc. Ch 3, (slip st, ch 3, slip st) in next (center) dc. Ch 3, slip st in next dc, ch 3, skip 2 dc, slip st in next sc. At end of round, slip st in same sc as beginning of round. Fasten off. Weave in ends. Block lightly.

STITCH KEY	
⬯	= chain (ch)
•	= slip stitch (slip st)
X	= single crochet (sc)
T	= half double crochet (hdc)
Ŧ	= double crochet (dc)
⸶	= treble crochet (tr)
⹀	= double treble crochet (dtr)
⌒	= worked in back loop

Candy Cane Afghan

We changed this afghan from a pink peppermint to a minty
green spearmint colorway. When making these round motifs, you
cleverly work one color over the other color for the color changes.
Note how even though phones have changed over the years, the
comfort of an afghan is still the same.

Adapted by
Marianne Forrestal

SIZES: *One size*

FINISHED MEASUREMENTS:
   45" × 60" (114cm × 152cm)

YARN:
6 skeins Red Heart® Eco-Ways® (acrylic/
   recycled polyester, 186 yds [170m]
   per 4 oz skein) in each of colors #3520
   Aquarium (A), #1600 Cotton (B)

HOOK: *Size J (6mm) crochet hook*

NOTIONS: *Yarn needle*

GAUGE: *Motif = 4½" (11cm) across*

> **NOTE:** *When changing color,*
> *work last st of old color until 2*
> *loops are left on hook, drop old*
> *color, yo with new color, and*
> *complete stitch. Work over color*
> *not in use. Be careful not to pull*
> *unused color too tightly or motif*
> *will pucker.*

Candy Cane Afghan

Afghan

Motif

Make 142.

Round 1: With A, ch 6, join with slip st to form a ring. Ch 3 (counts as first dc), 2 dc in ring, drop A, with B, 3 dc in ring, [drop B, with A, 3 dc in ring, drop A, with B, 3 dc in ring] twice, drop B, with A, join with slip st in top of starting ch-3—18 dc.

Round 2: With A, ch 3, dc in same space, 2 dc in next 2 dc, [change color, 2 dc in each of the next 3 dc] 5 times, change to A, join with slip st in top of starting ch-3—36 dc.

Round 3: With A, ch 3, dc in same space, dc in next 4 dc, 2 dc in next dc, [change color, 2 dc in next dc, dc in next 4 dc, 2 dc in next dc] 5 times, change to A, join with slip st in top of starting ch-3. Fasten off both A and B—48 dc.

Finishing

With WS facing, sew motifs together, joining half (4 sts) of an A section and half (4 sts) of a B section to corresponding sections on the next motif. Start with a row of 9 motifs, then a row of 10 motifs, then a row of 9 motifs, and so on, until there are 15 rows total, ending with a row of 9 motifs.

Edging

Work 1 round of sc around outside edge of throw, using A on the B sections and B on the A sections and working over color not in use. Join with a slip st to first sc. Fasten off and weave in ends.

Stitch Diagram

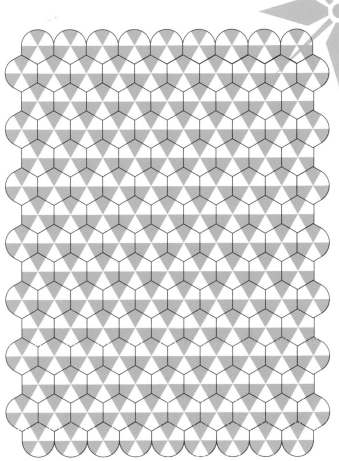

Assembly Diagram

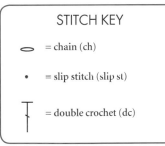

STITCH KEY

◯ = chain (ch)

• = slip stitch (slip st)

T = double crochet (dc)

EASY

Granny's Favorite Afghan

We're not sure why this was granny's favorite. Maybe she liked how colorful it was when she used a print yarn. Since it was her favorite, we decided not to change it too much.

Adapted by
Katherine Eng

SIZES: *One size*

FINISHED MEASUREMENTS:
   45" × 57½" (114cm × 146cm)

YARN:

5 skeins Red Heart® Super Saver® Prints (acrylic, 244 yds [233m] per 5 oz skein) in color #964 Primary (A)

3 skeins Red Heart® Super Saver® (acrylic, 364 yds [333m] per 7 oz skein) in color #387 Soft Navy (B)

HOOK: *Size J (6mm) crochet hook*

NOTIONS: *Yarn needle*

GAUGE: *Motif = 6" (15cm) square*

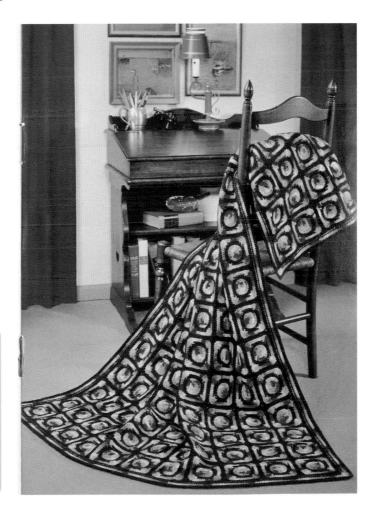

SPECIAL ABBREVIATION:

Fpdc (front post double crochet):
Yo, insert hook from front to back to front around post of specified st in row below, draw up loop, [yo and draw through 2 loops on hook] twice.

NOTE: *Always join with a slip st. When joining last st to ch-3 at beginning of rounds, slip st in 3rd ch. Work first st of next round in top of this ch.*

Granny's Favorite Afghan

Afghan

Motif

Make 63.

With A, ch 4, join. Ch 3 (counts as dc here and throughout).

Round 1: Work 11 dc in ring. Join to top of beginning ch-3—12 dc. Ch 3.

Round 2: Fpdc around dc (ch-3 at beginning of Round 1), * dc in next dc, fpdc around same dc; repeat from * around. Join and fasten off—12 dc and 12 fpdc.

With B, draw up a loop in first dc of Round 2. Ch 1.

Note: Work in each dc and in each fpdc around.

Round 3: Sc in same dc (ch 3 at beginning of round) and in next dc, * 2 sc in next dc, ** sc in each of next 2 dc; repeat from * around, ending at ** on last repeat. Join to beginning sc—32 sc. Ch 1.

Round 4: * Sc in next 5 sc, hdc in next sc, (dc, ch 2, dc) in next sc, hdc in next sc; repeat from * around. Join and fasten off.

With A, draw up a loop in any corner ch-2 space. Ch 3.

Round 5: 3 tr and dc in corner space, * fpdc around next dc, hdc, next 5 sc, next hdc, and next dc, ** (dc, 3 tr, and dc) in next corner space; repeat from * around, ending at ** on last repeat. Join to beginning dc and fasten off.

With B, draw up a loop in back loop of any dc. Ch 1.

Round 6: Working in back loops of sts only, sc in each st around, working (sc, ch 3, sc) in center of each corner 3-tr group. Join last sc to first and fasten off. Weave in ends.

Finishing

With B and RS facing, sew motifs together using a whipstitch through the back loops. Make 7 strips of 9 motifs each. Sew strips together.

Border

With B and RS facing, draw up a loop in 6th sc to the left of any corner ch-3 space. Ch 1.

Round 1 (RS): Sc in each sc, in each ch-3 space to the right of seam, in joining seam and in ch-3 space to the left of joining seam, working (sc, ch 3, sc) in each corner ch-3 space, join—161 sc each length and 125 each width. Ch 1, turn.

Round 2 (WS): Sc in next sc, * ch 1, skip 1 sc, sc in next sc; repeat from * around, working ch 1, skip 1 sc, (sc, ch 3, sc) in each corner ch-3 space. At end of round, join and fasten off.

With A and RS facing, draw up a loop in last sc of corner, ch 3.

Round 3 (RS): Dc in next ch-1 space and in each sc and ch-1 space around, working (2 dc, ch 3, 2 dc) in each corner ch-3 space. At end of round, join and fasten off.

With B and RS facing, draw up a loop in back loop of 6th dc to the left of any corner ch-3 space. Ch 1.

Round 4 (RS): Sc in back loop of each dc around, working (sc, ch 3, sc) in each corner ch-3 space. At end of round, join. Ch 1, turn.

Round 5 (WS): Repeat Round 2. At end of round, ch 1, turn.

Round 6 (RS): Sc in next ch-1 space and in each sc and ch-1 space around, working (sc, ch 3, sc) in each corner ch-3 space. At end of round, join and fasten off. Weave in ends. Block lightly.

Border

Stitch Diagram

STITCH KEY

⬭ = chain (ch)

• = slip stitch (slip st)

✕ = single crochet (sc)

⊤ = half double crochet (hdc)

† = double crochet (dc)

ⱡ = front post double crochet (fpdc)

† = treble crochet (tr)

⌒ = worked in back loop only

Checkmate Afghan & Pillow

The surprising thing about this updated Checkmate square is that it is started at the lower left corner and then worked to the opposite upper right corner. Hopefully, no one will really smoke a smelly pipe around this wonderful afghan.

Adapted by Katherine Eng

SIZES: *One size*

FINISHED MEASUREMENTS:

AFGHAN: *44" × 62" (112cm × 157cm)*

PILLOW: *18" (46cm) square*

YARN:

6 skeins Red Heart® Super Saver® (acrylic, 364 yds [333m] per 7 oz skein) in color #656 Real Teal (A)

4 skeins Red Heart® Super Saver® Prints (acrylic, 244 yds [233m] per 5 oz skein) in color #946 Peruvian Print (B)

HOOK: *Size H (5mm) crochet hook*

NOTIONS:

Yarn needle

18" (46cm) pillow form

GAUGE: *Large Square = 4¾" (12cm)*

·17·

105

Checkmate Afghan & Pillow

Afghan

Large Square 1

Small Square 1: Beginning at bottom left corner with B, ch 4.

Row 1 (RS): Sc in 2nd ch from hook, ch 1, skip 1 ch, sc in next ch. Ch 1, turn.

Row 2: Sc in first sc. Ch 1, skip next ch-1 space, sc in next sc. Ch 1, turn.

Row 3: Repeat Row 2. Fasten off.

Note: Work slip stitches to join only on RS rows, joining to square on the left.

Small Square 2: With A, ch 4 from 3rd ch of Square 1.

Row 1 (RS): Repeat Row 1 of Square 1, slip st in Row 1 of Square 1 to join. Ch 1, turn.

Row 2: Repeat Row 2 of Square 1.

Row 3: Repeat Row 3 of Square 1, slip st in Row 3 of Square 1. Ch 1.

Small Square 3: Work as for Row 2 of Small Square across top of Square 1 for 3 rows. Fasten off.

Continue adding small squares across from bottom to top on the diagonal, alternating colors with each row until there are 5 squares across, joining on RS rows to square on the left with a slip st as established and as shown on chart.

Then build squares across, starting on top of first square of last row of squares and ending at top square. Keep decreasing number of squares across until you have a block of 5 × 5 small squares.

NOTES: *Work both small and large squares from bottom to top across on the diagonal. Stitch pattern for Row 2 of Large Square is repeated throughout and referred to as "pattern st". Slip st as specified while working RS rows only to specified row of previous square on the left to join. Checkered 25-patch square (which makes up one Large Square) must be worked individually. Large solid color squares can be worked continuously across on the diagonal. Follow chart for clarity. When working in rounds, always join last st of round to first with a slip st.*

Large Square 2

With A, ch 20 from last bottom Small Square at bottom right corner of Square 1.

Row 1 (RS): Sc in second ch from hook, * ch 1, skip 1 ch, sc in next ch; repeat from * across. Ch 1, turn—10 sc and 9 ch-1 spaces. Slip st in Row 1 of same Small Square.

Row 2: Sc in first sc, * ch 1, skip next ch-1 space, sc in next sc; repeat from * across. Ch 1, turn.

Row 3: Repeat Row 2. Slip st in Row 3 of same Small Square. Ch 1, turn.

Continue in pattern st until 15 rows are completed, slip stitching to every other row on the left. At end of Row 15, ch 1.

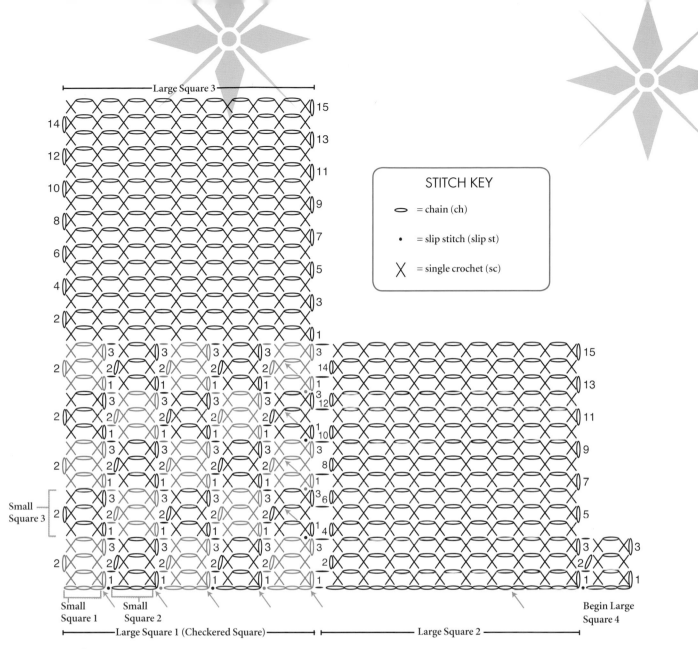

STITCH KEY

⬯ = chain (ch)

• = slip stitch (slip st)

✕ = single crochet (sc)

Large Square 3

Small Square 3

Small Square 1

Small Square 2

Large Square 1 (Checkered Square)

Large Square 2

Begin Large Square 4

Stitch Diagram

Checkmate Afghan & Pillow

Large Square 3

Work across top of beginning checkered square.

Row 1 (RS): Ch 1, sc in first sc, * ch 1, skip next ch-1 space (or next joining seam), sc in next sc; repeat from * across. Ch 1, turn—10 sc and 9 ch-1 spaces.

Rows 2-15: Work in pattern st. Fasten off.

Note: 3 Large Squares (1 checkered and 2 solid) completed.

Large Square 4

Work another full checkered square. Join B at bottom of first "A" square (Square 2) and begin another checkered square by working ch 4 from 19th ch of bottom Large Square, slip stitching to Rows 1 and 3, 4 and 6, 7 and 9, 10 and 12, and 13 and 15 of "A" square on the left.

Remaining Large Squares

Begin next checkered square on top of first large "A" square (Square 2). With B, draw up a loop in 2nd sc to the right of left hand edge. Ch 1. Slip stitching as on previous checkered square, work each small square beginning 2 sc over from last small square and skipping over ch-1 spaces between when slip stitching.

Work another checkered square across top of 2nd large "A" square (Square 3), beginning in 2nd sc from left hand edge.

Continue building alternate rows of squares until there are 9 diagonal squares across (last row is 9 checkered squares). Starting on top of checkered square at bottom right corner, work 9 "A" squares across. Repeat with checkered square, starting on top of "A" square and working 9 large squares across. Repeat both again. Then work alternating squares of 8, 7, 6, 5, 4, 3, 2, and 1 per row.

Finishing

Border:

With A and RS facing, draw up a loop in bottom right corner ch.

Round 1 (RS): Work up right hand side to top: * ch 2, skip 1 row, slip st in next row; repeat from * across, ending at top right corner with ch 2, (slip st, ch 3, slip st) in top sc. Work across top: ** ch 2, skip 1 st or ch-1 space, slip st in next st or ch-1 space; repeat from ** across top, ending with ch 2, skip last ch-1 space, (slip st, ch 3, slip st) in left hand top corner sc. Work down left hand side to bottom: *** ch 2, slip st in end of next row; repeat from *** across, ending at bottom left hand corner with ch 2, skip end of last row (Row 1 of beginning), (slip st, ch 3, slip st) in corner ch. Work across bottom: **** ch 2, skip 1 ch, slip st in next ch or ch-1 space; repeat from **** across, ending with ch 2, skip last ch, (slip st, ch 3, slip st) in bottom right corner ch. Fasten off. Weave in ends. Block lightly.

Pillow

Make 2.
Work as for Afghan until piece contains 9 Large Squares.

Finishing

Border:

Round 1 (RS): Work as for Round 1 of Afghan border. Do not fasten off. Slip st in next ch-2 space.

Round 2: * Ch 2, slip st in next ch-2 space; repeat from * around working at each corner: ch 2, (slip st, ch 3, slip st) in corner ch-3 space. At end of round, ch 2, slip st in slip st at end of round 1. Fasten off.

With B and RS facing, draw up a loop in a ch-2 space near center of either side. Ch 1.

Round 3 (RS): Sc in same space, * ch 1, sc in next ch-2 space; repeat from * around, working at each corner: ch 1, (sc, ch 2, sc) in corner ch-3 space. At end of round, join. Ch 1, turn.

Round 4 (WS): Sc in next ch-1 space, * ch 1, skip next sc, sc in next ch-1 space; repeat from * around, working at each corner: ch 1, skip next sc, (sc, ch 2, sc) in corner ch-2 space. At end of round, join. Ch 1, turn.

Rounds 5-6: Repeat Round 4. At end of Round 6, join and fasten off.

With A and RS facing, draw up a loop in a ch-1 space near center of opposite side. Ch 1.

Rounds 7-10: Repeat Round 4. At end of Round 10, join and fasten off.

Weave in ends. Block lightly. Place pieces with WS together.

With A, draw up a loop through ch-1 space of both pieces at first space to the left of any corner.

Note: On next round, join around 3 sides, insert pillow form and close last side.

Round 11 (RS): * Ch 2, skip next sc, slip st in next ch-1 space; repeat from * around, working at each corner: ch 2, skip next sc, (slip st, ch 2, slip st) in corner ch-2 space. At end of round, slip st in beginning space and fasten off. Weave in ends.

Maltese Cross Afghan & Pillow

The new rendition of the Maltese Cross looks like a flower garden. With two shades of yarn for the first two rounds of all squares and then purple, lavender, orchid or pale plum for the third round, it's a floral beauty.

Adapted by Katherine Eng

SIZES: *One size*

FINISHED MEASUREMENTS:

AFGHAN: *46½ × 56½" (118cm × 144cm)*

PILLOW: *18" (46cm) square*

YARN:

4 skeins Red Heart® Super Saver® (acrylic, 364 yds [333m] per 7 oz skein) in color #631 Light Sage (A)

2 skeins Red Heart® Super Saver® (acrylic, 364 yds [333m] per 7 oz skein) in color #320 Cornmeal (B)

1 skein Red Heart® Super Saver® (acrylic, 364 yds [333m] per 7 oz skein) in each of colors #528 Medium Purple (C), #358 Lavender (D), #579 Pale Plum (E), #530 Orchid (F)

HOOK: *Size J (6mm) crochet hook*

NOTIONS:

Yarn needle

18" (46cm) pillow form

2- 18½" (47cm) square pieces of white felt

GAUGE: *Motif = 4" (10cm) square*

Maltese Cross Afghan & Pillow

SPECIAL ABBREVIATION & STITCH:

Ldc (long dc): Work dc into space indicated, pulling loop even with loop on hook; complete st as usual.
Shell: 5 dc in same space

NOTE: *On Round 3 of each motif, change colors as follows: 59 motifs with C, 20 with D, 28 with F, and 36 with E. Always join last st of round to first with a slip st. Except where specified, work through both loops of sts.*

Afghan

Motif

Make 143: 59 with C, 20 with D, 28 with F, and 36 with E.

With A, ch 4, join. Ch 1.

Round 1: Work 8 sc in ring, join and fasten off. With B, draw up a loop in first sc of Round 1, ch 3 (counts as first dc of Round 2).

Round 2: Dc in same sc, 2 dc in next sc, * ch 3, ** 2 dc in each of next 2 sc; repeat from * around, ending at ** on last repeat. Join to beginning dc (3rd ch of beginning ch). Fasten off.

With C (D, E, or F), draw up a loop in top of beginning dc of Round 2 (top of 3rd ch). Ch 1.

Round 3: Sc in same ch and in back loop of next 3 dc, * ldc over ch-3 (corner) into "A" sc of Round 1 where last dc of "B" group was made, ch 3, ldc over ch-3 space in next "A" sc, ** sc in back loop of next 4 dc; repeat from * around, ending at ** on last repeat. Join to beginning sc. Fasten off.

With A, draw up a loop in any corner space. Ch 1.

Round 4: * (2 sc, dc, and 2 sc) in ch-3 space, sc in back loop of next 6 sts; repeat from * around. Join and fasten off.

Finishing

Weave in ends. With A and RS facing, sew motifs together in 11 rows of 13 motifs each using a whipstitch as shown on page 114, then sew strips together.

Row 1: 13 C.
Row 2: 1 C, 11 E, 1 C.
Row 3: 1 C, 1 E, 9 F, 1 E, 1 C.
Row 4: 1 C, 1 E, 1 F, 7 D, 1 F, 1 E, 1 C.
Row 5: 1 C, 1 E, 1 F, 1 D, 5 C, 1 D, 1 F, 1 E, 1 C.
Row 6: Repeat Row 5.
Rows 7-11: Repeat Rows 5-1 (work backward).

Border

With A and RS facing, draw up a loop in a sc near center of motif next to any corner. Ch 1.

Round 1 (RS): Sc in each sc, hdc in each dc and dc in each joining seam around, working at each corner: hdc in sc before corner dc, (hdc, ch 2, hdc) in corner dc, hdc in next sc. At end of round, join. Ch 1, turn—168 sts each side and 142 sts top and bottom.

Round 2 (WS): Sc in next sc and in each st around, working (sc, ch 2, sc) in each corner ch-2 space. Join and fasten off.

With D and RS facing, draw up a loop in any sc on side edge away from corner. Ch 3 (counts as first dc of Round 3).

Round 3: Dc in each sc around, working (2 dc, ch 2, 2 dc) in each corner ch-2 space. Join last dc to first (top of ch-3). Fasten off.

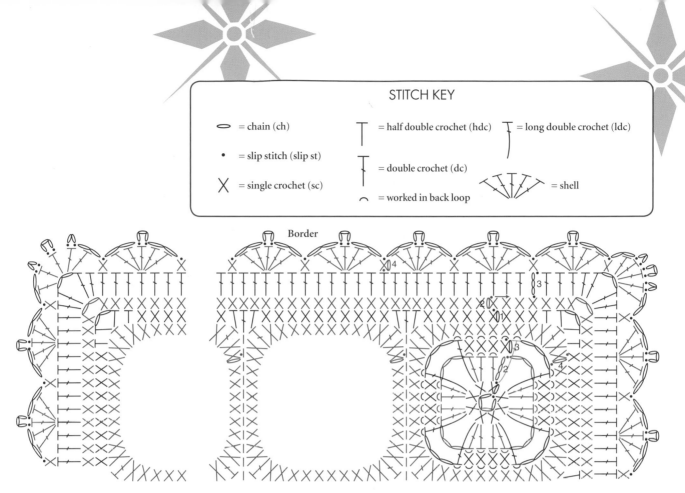

○ = chain (ch)

• = slip stitch (slip st)

✕ = single crochet (sc)

T = half double crochet (hdc)

T = double crochet (dc)

⌒ = worked in back loop

ꟼ = long double crochet (ldc)

= shell

Border

Stitch Diagram

With A and RS facing, draw up a loop in 18th dc to the left of corner on either side edge. Ch 1.

Round 4: Sc in same dc, * skip 2 dc, shell in next dc, skip 2 dc, sc in next dc; repeat from * around, working at corners 1 and 3: shell in corner ch-2 space, skip 1 dc, sc in next dc. At corners 2 and 4: skip 2 dc, shell and sc in corner ch-2 space. At end of round, join last shell to beginning sc. Fasten off. With C and RS facing, draw up a loop in a sc on any edge between 2 shells and away from corner.

Round 5: * Ch 2, (slip st, ch 3, slip st) in center dc of next shell, ch 2, slip st in next sc; repeat from * around, working at each corner: ch 2, skip 1 dc, (slip st, ch 2, slip st) in next dc, (slip st, ch 3, slip st) in next dc, (slip st, ch 2, slip st) in next dc, ch 2, skip 1 dc, slip st in next sc. At end of round, work last slip st in same sc as beginning. Fasten off. Weave in ends. Block lightly.

Maltese Cross Afghan & Pillow

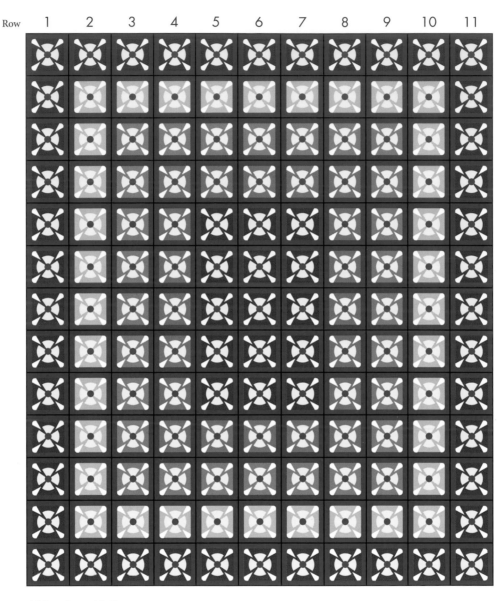

Afghan Assembly Diagram

Pillow

Make 32 motifs, 8 each of colors C, D, E, F.

Finishing

Assemble as for Afghan as shown at right.

Row 1: 2 F, 2 E.

Row 2: 1 D, 2 C, 1 D.

Row 3: Repeat Row 2.

Row 4: 2 E, 2 F.

Work Border Rounds 1-3 of Afghan around each piece, using C on Round 3 (instead of D). Weave in ends. Block lightly. Sew squares of felt together on 3 sides, using a ¼" (6mm) seam. Turn inside out. Insert pillow form, turn remaining edges in and sew closed. Place crocheted pieces together with WS together. With A, draw up a loop through both corner ch-2 spaces to join. Ch 1.

Next Round: Work around 3 sides as follows through both thicknesses, then insert pillow form and complete last side: ([sc, ch 2] twice, sc) in corner space, * skip 1 sc, (sc, ch 2, sc) in next dc; * repeat from * around, working corner pattern in each corner ch-2 space. Join and fasten off. Weave in ends.

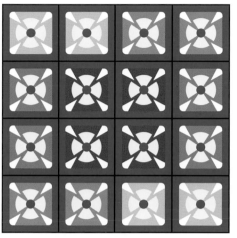

Pillow Assembly Diagram

Shaded Stripes Afghan

The curlicue fringe is surprisingly not a new invention. Creative designers adapt the old ideas to new style and color sensibilities as shown here in this old (upper left in vintage image) to new creation.

*Adapted by
Mary Jane Protus*

SIZES: *One size*

FINISHED MEASUREMENTS:

    *44" × 60" (112cm × 152cm),
excluding spiral fringe*

YARN:

*4 skeins Red Heart® Super Saver®
(acrylic, 364 yds [333m] per 7 oz
skein) in color #316 Soft White (A)*

*3 skeins Red Heart® Super Saver®
(acrylic, 364 yds [333m] per 7 oz
skein) in color #656 Real Teal (B)*

*2 skeins Red Heart® Super Saver®
(acrylic, 364 yds [333m] per 7 oz
skein) in each of colors #505 Aruba
Sea (C), #512 Turqua (D)*

HOOK: *Size K (6.5mm) crochet hook*

NOTIONS: *Yarn needle*

GAUGE: *11 sc and 12 rows = 4"
(10cm)*

SPECIAL ABBREVIATION:

*Fpdc (front post double crochet):
Yo, insert hook from front to back
to front around post of specified st
in row below, draw up loop, [yo and
draw through 2 loops on hook] twice.*

NOTE: *When working fpdc, skip the st directly behind the post st before
making the next st throughout.*

Shaded Stripes Afghan

Afghan

With A, ch 122.

Row 1: Hdc in 3rd ch from hook (turning ch counts as a st) and in each ch across; turn—121 hdc.

Row 2 (RS): Ch 1, sc in first hdc, * fpdc around next hdc of previous row, sc in next hdc; repeat from * across; turn.

Rows 3 and 5: Ch 1, sc in first st and in each st across, turn—121 sc.

Rows 4 and 6: Ch 1, sc in first sc, * fpdc around next st in previous dc row, sc in next sc; repeat from * across; turn. At end of Row 6, change to C in last st.

Repeat Rows 3 and 4 for pattern and, at the same time, begin Stripe Sequences as follows:

Stripe Sequence A (10 rows): Work 2 rows each of C, D, B, D, C.

Join A and work 6 rows in established pattern.

Stripe Sequence B (10 rows): Work 2 rows each of C, B, D, B, C.

Join A and work 6 rows in established pattern. Continue working Rows 3 and 4 for pattern, and, at the same time, continue working the following stripe sequence [Stripe Sequence A, 6 rows A, Stripe Sequence B, 6 rows A] four times, work Stripe A once more, work 6 rows A, fasten off.

Finishing

Border

Round 1 (RS): Join B in top right-hand corner, ch 1, work (sc, ch 1, sc) (CORNER made) in first sc of last row worked (top of afghan), sc evenly along each side, working CORNER in each corner, join with slip st in first sc, slip st into ch-1 space.

Round 2: * Ch 15, work 2 sc in 2nd ch from hook and in each ch across—28 sc (SPIRAL FRINGE made), skip next sc on afghan, sc in next 3 sc of afghan; repeat from * across to ch-1 space; make one more SPIRAL FRINGE, skip ch-1 space. Slip st in each sc along side to ch-1 space of next corner; repeat same along bottom and next side; join with a slip st in beginning slip st, fasten off.

Weave in ends.

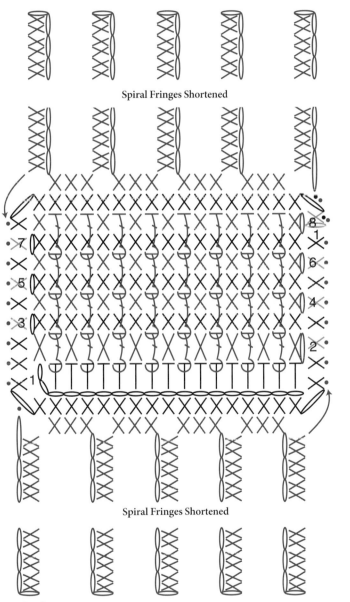

Spiral Fringes Shortened

Spiral Fringes Shortened

Stitch Diagram

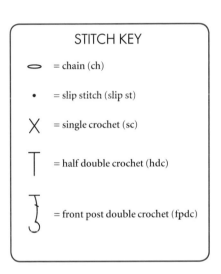

STITCH KEY

$\bigcirc$ = chain (ch)

$\bullet$ = slip stitch (slip st)

$\times$ = single crochet (sc)

$\top$ = half double crochet (hdc)

$\mathbf{J}$ = front post double crochet (fpdc)

Tweedy Square Pillows

Not only do the stitches used for these pillows give them a tweedy look, but one of the pillows is actually made with a tweedy flecked yarn. They're perfectly buttoned to give your modern home a bit of mid-century flair.

Adapted by
Alexis Williams

SIZES: *One size*

FINISHED MEASUREMENTS:

16" (41cm) square

YARN:

TWEED VERSION

2 skeins Red Heart® Fiesta® (acrylic/ nylon, 316 yds [289m] per 6 oz skein) in color #6400 Platinum

SOLID VERSION

2 skeins Red Heart® Super Saver® (acrylic, 364 yds [333m] per 7 oz skein) in color #332 Ranch Red

HOOK: *Size I (5.5mm) crochet hook*

NOTIONS:

16" (41cm) pillow form

2" (5cm) button

Yarn needle

GAUGE:

TWEED VERSION

14 sts and 6 rows = 4" (10cm)

SOLID VERSION

14 sts and 5 rows = 4" (10cm)

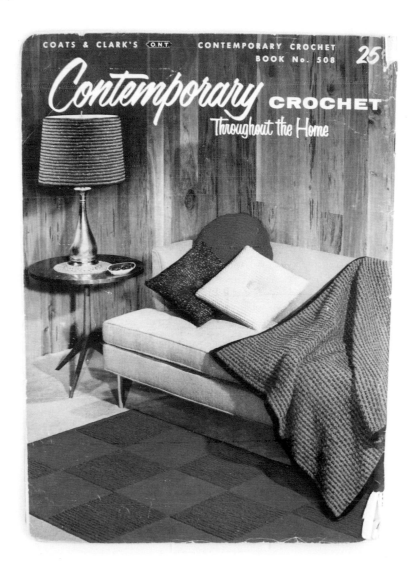

Tweedy Square Pillows

Pillow

Front and Back

Make 2.

Tweed Version

Ch 57.

Row 1 (RS): Sc in 2nd ch from hook and in each ch across—56 sc. Ch 1, turn.

Row 2: Sc in first sc, skip next 2 sc, * tr in next sc, sc in each of the 2 skipped sc, skip next 2 free sc; repeat from * across, ending with sc in last sc. Ch 1, turn.

Row 3: 2 sc in first sc (1 sc increase), sc in each sc across to last 2 sc, decrease 1 sc (sc 2 together), ch 1, turn.

Repeat Rows 2 and 3 for pattern until piece measures approximately 16" (41cm). Fasten off.

Solid Version

Ch 58.

Row 1 (RS): 2 dc in 3rd ch from hook, *skip 2 ch, (sc, 2 dc) in next chain; repeat from *, ending with skip 2 ch, sc in last ch. Ch 2, turn.

Row 2: 2 dc in first sc, *skip 2 dc, (sc, 2 dc) in next sc; repeat from *, ending with sc in top of turning ch. Ch 2, turn.

Repeat Row 2 for pattern, until piece measures approximately 16" (41cm). Fasten off.

Finishing

Weave in ends. With WS together, sew pillow front and back together on 3 sides. Insert pillow form, sew last side closed. Sew button through pillow at center front.

Stitch Diagram 1, Tweed Version

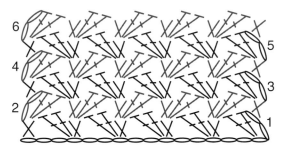

Stitch Diagram 2, Solid Version

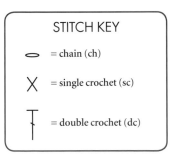

STITCH KEY

⬭ = chain (ch)

X = single crochet (sc)

T = double crochet (dc)

Crochet Basics

Whether you are using a crochet hook for the first time or just need a refresher course, we've included all the basics for successful crocheting. You'll find information on tools, *materials, crochet stitches and how to work from a stitch diagram.*

This chapter will help prepare you to tackle any project you desire.

Tools and Materials

Crochet Hooks

Hooks are usually made from steel, aluminum or plastic in a range of sizes according to their diameter. Hooks are also available in wood and bamboo. If you are having difficulty obtaining gauge or working smoothly with a particular type of yarn, consider changing the type of hook you are using.

Standard Yarn Weight System

Categories of yarn, gauge ranges and recommended hook sizes

Yarn Weight Symbol & Category Names	1 Super Fine	2 Fine	3 Light	4 Medium	5 Bulky	6 Super Bulky
Type of Yarns in Category	Sock, Fingering, Baby	Sport, Baby	DK, Light Worsted	Worsted, Afghan, Aran	Chunky, Craft, Rug	Bulky, Roving
Crochet Gauge Range* (Single Crochet - 4"/10 cm)	21 - 32 sts	16 - 20 sts	12 - 17 sts	11 - 14 sts	8 - 11 sts	5 - 9 sts
Recommended Hook in Metric Size Range	2.25 - 3.5 mm	3.5 - 4..5 mm	4.5 - 5.5 mm	5.5 - 6.5 mm	6.5 - 9 mm	9 mm and larger
Recommended Hook in U.S. Size Range	B-1 - E-4	E-4 - 7	7 - I-9	I-9 - K-10½	K-10½ - M-13	M-13 and larger

* GUIDELINES ONLY: The above reflect the most commonly used gauges and hook sizes for specific yarn categories.

The six standardized yarn weight groups as defined by the Craft Yarn Council of America.

Thread Weight System

Categories of crochet thread, gauge ranges and recommended hook sizes

Thread Weight Symbol	EXTRA FINE 30 TRÉS FIN MUY FINO	FINE 20 FIN FINO	CLASSIC 10 CLASSIQUE CLÁSICO	FASHION 5 MODE MODA	FASHION 3 MODE MODA
Crochet Stitch Gauge (Single Crochet - 4"/10 cm)	56 - 60	46 - 52	32 - 42	29 - 34	16 - 21
Crochet Row Gauge (Single Crochet - 4"/10 cm)	22 - 32	20 - 24	15 - 20	14 - 16	8 - 10
Recommended Hook in Metric Size Range	1.0 mm	1.15 - 1.25 mm	1.4 - 1.5 mm	1.75 mm	3.5 mm
Recommended Hook in U.S. Size Range	11 - 12	9 - 10	7 - 8	4	D-3

Other Handy Tools

You'll find these tools helpful—yarn needles and plastic seaming pins (that don't split the yarn when they're inserted into stitches), a measuring tape, metal gauge, sharp scissors, Post-It® notes (for marking your place in the pattern and for jotting down notes as you're stitching) and split-ring stitch markers for marking stitches or rows in the crocheted fabric.

Yarn and Thread

Yarns are available in a variety of weights. When talking about yarn, *weight* means the thickness of the strand of yarn.

Yarn comes in either a long center-pull skein or a ball. The pull skein lets you pull your working yarn from the center while a ball is used starting from the outside.

Threads are available in several weights with the most popular being size 10, often referred to as bedspread weight. The thread projects in this book have been made with cotton thread in sizes 10 and 3, and bamboo thread in size 10.

Holding the Hook and Yarn

There are no hard and fast rules about the best way to hold the hook and yarn. Choose whichever way you find the most comfortable.

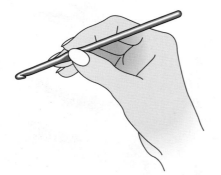

Some people prefer the pencil grip. The hook is held in the right hand as if holding a pencil.

First Steps

To learn to crochet, we suggest you use a medium worsted weight yarn and a 5mm (US H-8) or 5.5mm (US I-9) hook.

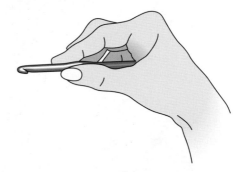

Another hold is the knife grip. The hook is held in the right hand as if holding a dinner knife ready to cut.

To maintain the slight tension in the yarn necessary for easy, even stitches, you may find it helpful to wrap the yarn around the fingers of the hand opposite the one holding the hook. Try one of these ways, or find another way that feels comfortable to you.

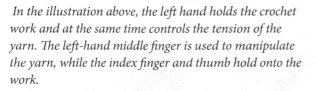

In the illustration above, the left hand holds the crochet work and at the same time controls the tension of the yarn. The left-hand middle finger is used to manipulate the yarn, while the index finger and thumb hold onto the work.

You may find it more comfortable to manipulate the yarn with the index finger and hold the project with your thumb and middle finger. While you're learning, if one ways feels awkward, try another way until you find the one that suits you.

Basic Stitches

Almost all crochet begins with a base or foundation chain, which is a series of chain stitches, beginning with a slip knot.

Slip Knot

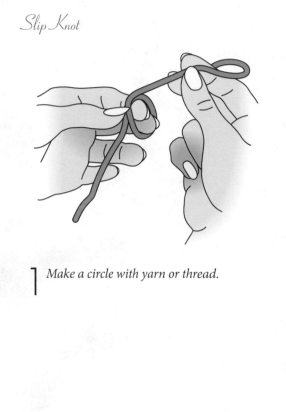

1 *Make a circle with yarn or thread.*

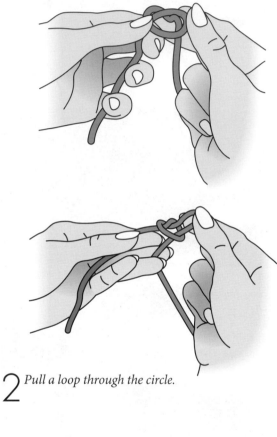

2 *Pull a loop through the circle.*

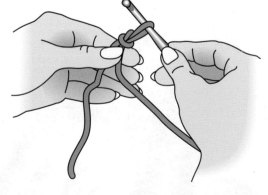

3 *Insert the hook in the loop.*

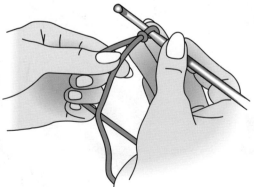

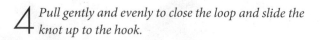

4 *Pull gently and evenly to close the loop and slide the knot up to the hook.*

Yarn Over (yo)

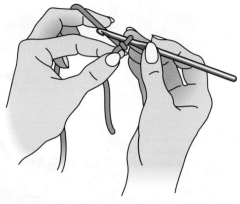

Wrap the yarn from back to front over the hook (or hold the yarn still and maneuver the hook). This movement of the yarn over the hook is used over and over again in crochet and is usually called "yarn over," abbreviated as yo.

Chain Stitch (ch)

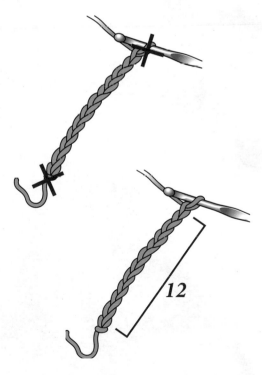

1 *Yarn over and pull the yarn through the loop already on the hook to form a new loop. Be careful not to tighten the previous loop.*

2 *Repeat Step 1 to form the number of chains specified in the instructions. Do not count the slip knot or the loop on the hook as a stitch.*

Working Into the Foundation Chain

When working into the starting chain, you may work under one or two strands of chain loops as shown at right. Either of these methods forms an even, firm bottom edge.

You may like to work into the "bump" on the back of the chain. This forms an even, stretchy bottom edge that is ideal for garments.

Whichever method of working into the foundation you choose, be consistent. Work all the pieces of a project in the same manner.

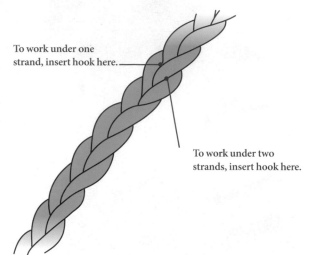

To work under one strand, insert hook here.

To work under two strands, insert hook here.

Basic Stitches

Whether the following basic stitches are worked into a starting chain or worked into a previous row, the method is the same.

• Slip Stitch (slip st)

This is the shortest of all crochet stitches. Unlike other stitches, slip stitches are not usually used on their own to produce a fabric. The slip stitch is used for joining, shaping and, where necessary, moving the yarn to another part of the fabric for the next stage.

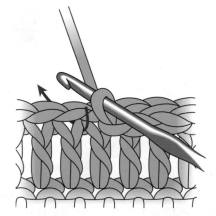

1 Insert the hook into the work as directed in pattern.

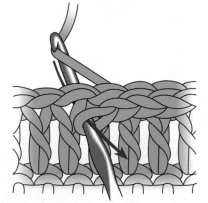

2 Yarn over and pull the yarn through in one movement. When working into previous rows, yarn over and pull the yarn through both the work and the loop on the hook in one movement.

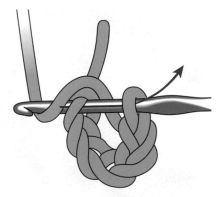

3 To join a chain ring with a slip stitch, insert the hook into the first chain, yarn over and pull the yarn through the work and the loop on the hook.

X Single Crochet (sc)

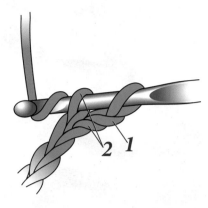

1 Insert the hook into the work (second chain from the hook on the starting chain), * yarn over and pull up a loop.

2 Yarn over again and pull the yarn through both loops on the hook.

3 1 sc made. Insert hook into the next stitch; repeat from * in Step 1.

Half Double Crochet (hdc)

1 Yarn over and insert the hook into the work (third chain from the hook on the starting chain).

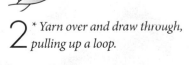

2 * Yarn over and draw through, pulling up a loop.

3 Yarn over again and pull the yarn through all three loops on the hook.

4 1 hdc made. Yarn over, insert hook into the next stitch; repeat from * in Step 2.

⊤ Double Crochet (dc)

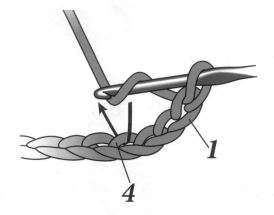

1 *Yarn over and insert the hook into the work (fourth chain from the hook on the starting chain).*

2 ** Yarn over and draw yarn through, pulling up a loop.*

3 *Yarn over and pull the yarn through the first two loops only on the hook.*

4 *Yarn over and pull the yarn through the last two loops on the hook.*

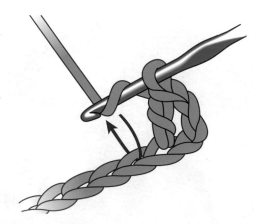

5 *1 dc made. Yarn over, insert hook into the next stitch; repeat from * in Step 2.*

T Treble (tr)

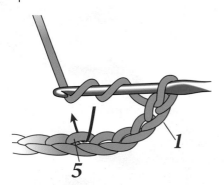

1 Yarn over twice and insert the hook into the work (fifth chain from hook on the starting chain).

2 *Yarn over and draw the yarn through, pulling up a loop.

3 Yarn over again and pull the yarn through the first two loops only on the hook.

4 Yarn over again and pull the yarn through the next two loops only on the hook.

5 Yarn over again and pull the yarn through the last two loops on the hook.

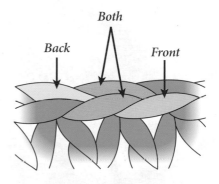

6 1 tr made. Yarn over twice, insert hook into the next stitch; repeat from * in Step 2.

Longer Basic Stitches

Double treble (dtr), triple treble (ttr), quadruple treble (qtr) etc., are made by wrapping the yarn over three, four, five times, etc., at the beginning and finishing as for a treble crochet, repeating Step 4 until two loops remain on the hook, and then finishing with Step 5.

Back Loop and Front Loop

The project instructions may specify if you are to work into the front or back loop of the stitch in the row below. Unless otherwise stated, always work under two strands of the top of the stitch in the row below.

Both

Back   Front

Making Crochet Fabric

Starting Chain

To make a flat crocheted fabric worked in rows, you must begin with a starting chain. The length of the starting chain is the number of stitches needed for the first row of fabric plus the number of chains needed to get to the correct height of the first stitch used in the first row.

Working in Rows

When working in rows, right-handers work from right to left and left-handers work from left to right, turning the work at the end of each row. One or more chains are worked at the beginning of each row to bring the hook up to the height of the first stitch in the row. The number of chains used for turning (called a turning chain in patterns) will depend upon the height of the stitch they are to match:

single crochet = 1 chain

half double crochet = 2 chains

double crochet = 3 chains

treble = 4 chains

When working half double crochet or longer stitches, the turning chain usually takes the place of the first stitch (the project instructions will let you know if the turning chains are not considered a stitch). When one chain is worked at the beginning of a row starting with a single crochet stitch, it is usually for height only and is made in addition to the first stitch.

Basic Double Crochet Fabric

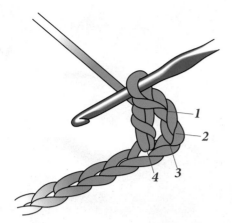

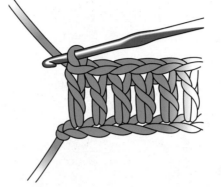

1 Make a starting chain of the required length plus two chains. Work one double crochet into the fourth chain from hook. The three chains at the beginning of the row form the first double crochet.

2 Work one double crochet into the next chain and every chain to the end of the row.

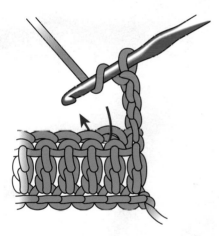

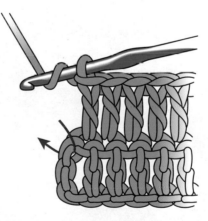

3 At the end of each crochet row, turn the work so that another row can be crocheted across the top of the previous row. It does not matter which way the work is turned, but be consistent. Make three chains for turning (which are then counted as the first double crochet). Skip the first double crochet in the previous row, work a double crochet into the top of the next and every double crochet including the last double crochet in row.

4 Work the last double crochet into the third of three chains at the beginning of the previous row.

Increasing and Decreasing

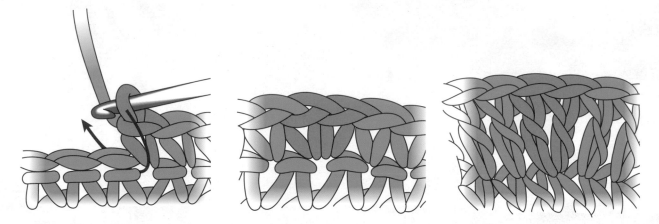

To increase the width of a basic crochet fabric, 2 or more stitches have to be worked into 1 stitch at the point specified in the project instructions. Single crochet, half double crochet, double crochet and longer stitches are all increased in this manner.

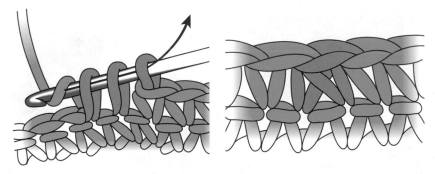

To decrease the width of a basic fabric, 2 or more stitches have to be worked together by leaving the last loop of each stitch on the hook then working them off together. Single crochet, half double crochet, and longer stitches can be decreased in this way, called sc2tog, hdc2tog, etc.

To decrease in single crochet, draw up a loop in each of the next 2 stitches, yarn over and pull the yarn through all three loops on the hook.

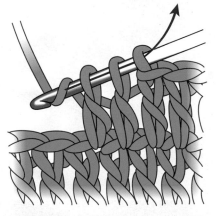

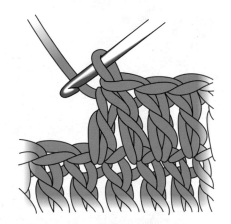

To decrease in double crochet, yarn over and draw up a loop in the next stitch, yarn over and pull the yarn through two loops only on the hook, yarn over and draw up a loop in the next stitch, yarn over and pull the yarn through two loops only on the hook, yarn over and pull the yarn through the remaining three loops on the hook.

Fastening Off

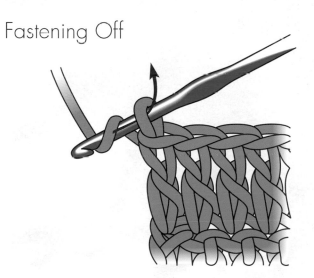

To fasten off the yarn permanently, cut the yarn leaving an 8" (20cm) end (longer if you need to sew pieces together). Pull the end of the yarn through the loop on the hook and pull gently to tighten.

Joining in New Yarn and Changing Colors

When joining in new yarn or changing color, continue in the working yarn until two loops of the last stitch remain in the working yarn or color.

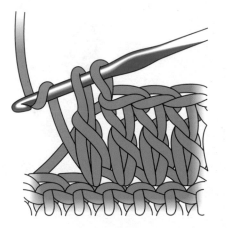

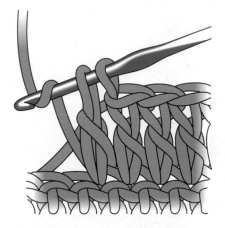

1 *Yarn over with the new color or yarn and pull the new color or yarn through to complete the stitch.*

2 *Continue to work the following stitches in the new color of yarn following the pattern instructions.*

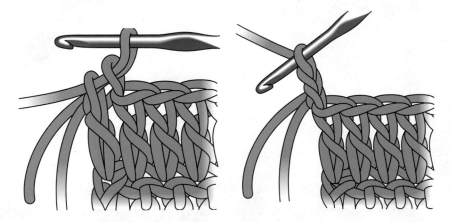

If you are working whole rows in different colors, make the change during the last stitch in the previous row, so the new color for the next row is ready to work the turning chain.

If you are working a narrow stripe pattern, instead of cutting off the old color or yarn, carry it loosely along the side of the fabric so that it is ready to pick up again the next time it is needed. For wide stripe patterns, it is usually best to cut off the old color or yarn, leaving a 6" (15cm) end for weaving in. Longer carries, or floats, are easily snagged.

Working in Rounds

Most motifs are not worked in rows but are worked in rounds from the center out. Unless otherwise stated in the pattern instructions, do not turn the work between rounds but continue with the same side facing and treat this as the right side (RS) of the fabric. The center ring is usually formed by a number of chains joined together with a slip stitch to form a ring.

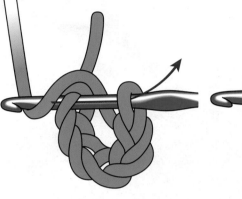

1 *Insert the hook into the first chain made.*

2 *Make a slip stitch to join the chains into a ring.*

3 *At the beginning of each round, one or more chain(s) can be worked to match the height of the following stitches. (This is equal to a turning chain.) When working in double crochet, three starting chains are required.*

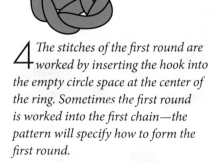

4 *The stitches of the first round are worked by inserting the hook into the empty circle space at the center of the ring. Sometimes the first round is worked into the first chain—the pattern will specify how to form the first round.*

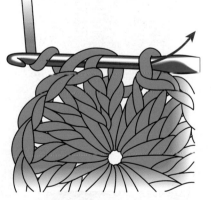

5 *When each round is complete, insert the hook into the top of the chain or stitch at the beginning of the round and make a slip stitch to close the round.*

6 *When working the second and subsequent rounds, unless otherwise stated, insert the hook under the two top loops of the stitches in the previous round.*

  After joining the final round with a slip stitch, fasten off by making one chain, then cutting the yarn and drawing the end through. Pull gently to tighten and form a knot.

Stitch Variations

Most crochet stitch patterns, no matter how complex they seem, are made using combinations of basic stitches. Different effects can be created by small variations in the stitch-making procedure or by varying the position and manner of inserting the hook into the fabric.

Note: Many patterns refer to certain groups of stitches in the instructions, but be careful—"bobble", "cluster", "shell", etc., may not mean the same thing from pattern to pattern. Always read the instructions carefully. Notes at the beginning of the pattern are important to read.

Reading a Crochet Pattern

In order to follow crochet instructions, you should know how to make the basic stitches and be familiar with basic fabric-making procedures. You should also be familiar with the abbreviations for the basic stitches.

Working from a Diagram

Diagrams should be read exactly as the crochet is worked. Each stitch is represented by a symbol that has been drawn to resemble its crocheted equivalent. The position of the symbol shows where the stitch should be worked.

Stitch symbols are drawn and laid out as realistically as possible, but there are times when they have to be distorted for the sake of clarity. For example, stitches may look extra long to show clearly where they are to be placed, but you should not try to match the chart by making elongated stitches. Crochet each stitch as you normally would.

Basic Symbols Used in Diagrams

Shown below are the standard symbols used for crochet stitch diagrams. If a pattern has an unusual stitch combination, there may be a special symbol, identified in the Stitch Key, for that design.

⌒	= Chain	T	= Half Double Crochet
•	= Slip Stitch	Ŧ	= Double Crochet
X	= Single Crochet	Ŧ	= Treble Crochet

Right Side and Wrong Side Rows

Where the work is turned after each row, only alternate rows are worked with the right side of the work facing. These "right side rows" are printed in black on stitch diagrams and read from right to left. Wrong side rows are printed in a different color (usually blue) and read from left to right. Row numbers are shown at the side of the diagrams at the beginning of the row.

Patterns worked in rounds have right side rows facing on every round—alternate rounds are printed in blue and black.

Pattern Repeats

In the written instructions, the stitches that should be repeated are contained within brackets [ ] or follow an asterisk *. These stitches are repeated across the row or round the required number of times. On diagrams, the stitches that have to be repeated can be easily visualized. The extra stitches not included in the pattern repeat are there to balance the row or make it symmetrical and are only worked once. Turning chains are only worked at the beginning of each row.

Gauge

Gauge is the number of stitches (and spaces) per inch and the number of rows (or rounds) per inch. Your gauge and the gauge listed at the beginning of the pattern should be the same so that your project will finish to the correct size and so you will not run out of yarn.

Before starting your pattern, check your gauge! Using the same yarn, hook or needle and pattern stitch specified in the instructions, make a swatch that is approximately 6" (15cm) square.

Using pins, mark off a section of stitches in the center of the swatch that measures 4" (10cm) square. Count the number of stitches and rows in this 4" (10cm) section. If they match the gauge, you can start right in on your pattern. If you have too few stitches, you are working too loosely—change to a smaller hook or needle size and make another swatch. If you have too many stitches, you are working too tightly—change to a larger hook or needle size and make another swatch.

The hook size stated in the pattern is a suggested hook size only. You must use whichever hook gives you the correct gauge.

Abbreviations and Symbols

Listed below are the standard abbreviations and symbols that are used in this book. If a pattern contains unusual combinations of stitches, these are explained in the Special Abbreviations section at the beginning of the pattern.

Abbreviations

A, B, C, etc.	Color A, Color B, Color C, etc.
ch(s)	chain(s)
cm	centimeter(s)
dec	decrease
dc	double crochet
dtr	double treble crochet
hdc	half double crochet
inc	increase
mm	millimeter(s)
rnd(s)	round(s)
RS	right side
sc	single crochet
sk	skip
sl	slip
sp(s)	space(s)
st(s)	stitch(es)
tr	treble crochet
WS	wrong side
yo	yarn over
* or **	repeat whatever follows the * or ** as indicated
[ ]	work directions in brackets the number of times indicated

Finishing

Weaving in Ends

Weave in ends securely before blocking pieces or sewing seams. Securely woven ends will not come loose with wear or washing. It's best to work in ends as invisibly as possible.

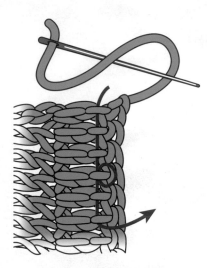

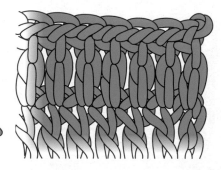

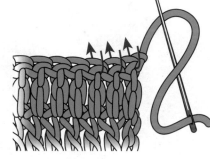

1 *Thread the yarn end through a blunt yarn needle. Whipstitch the end around several stitches. Trim the end close to the work.*

2 *The woven end should be nearly invisible.*

3 *Another method of weaving in ends is to run the end under several stitches, wrap it around a stitch and then run it under several more stitches. For even more security, reverse the direction and weave back under and over a few more stitches. Trim the end close to the work.*

Joining Seams

Various methods can be used to join pieces of crochet and, again, the use of the finished item often dictates the assembly method. Sewn seams can be invisible or decorative. Below are a few suggestions for joining pieces of crochet.

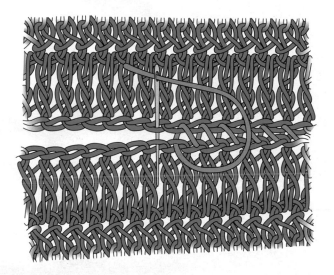

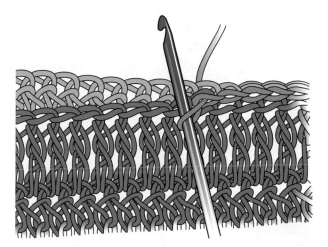

To join with an invisible sewn seam, place pieces edge to edge with the wrong sides facing up and whipstitch together.

To join invisibly using a crochet hook, place right sides of pieces together and slip stitch through one loop of each piece as illustrated.

Index

More crochet books you'll love

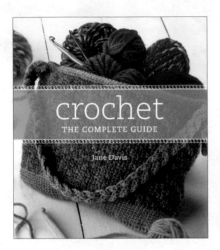

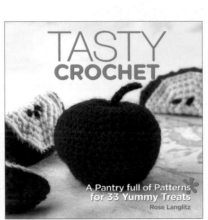

Crochet:
The Complete Guide

Jane Davis

It's amazing that a simple hook and yarn can yield such diverse results, from thick, cozy afghans to delicate lace doilies. Crochet The Complete Guide contains everything you need to get started or take your projects to the next level—from advice on selecting the best yarn types and colors for your projects, to easy-to-follow instructions for creating sophisticated edgings, lacework and three-dimensional textures, to multi-color effects, ruffles, flowers and much more!

hardcover with spiral binding; 5.625" × 7.625"; 256 pages
ISBN-10: 0-89689-697-8
ISBN-13: 978-0-89689-697-0
SRN: Z2345

Tasty Crochet
A Pantry Full of Patterns for 33 Yummy Treats

Rose Langlitz

Whether you're craving peanuts or pizza, you'll find just the thing to hit the spot between the covers of Tasty Crochet. With over 30 crochet patterns on the menu, there's something here to please every taste. In addition to snack items that can be stitched up in a flash, you'll find patterns for foods such as apples, ice cream sandwiches, tacos and more. A basic crochet techniques section gets you started right away or provides a great way to brush up on your skills.

paperback; 8" × 8"; 144 pages
ISBN-10: 1-60061-312-8
ISBN-13: 978-1-60061-312-8
SRN: Z2914

Crochet Now!
20 Projects for Baby, Home, Gifts and More

Candi Jensen

Get crocheting now with patterns from the first three seasons of PBS television show Knit & Crochet Now! Author and TV producer Candi Jensen brings you 29 fabulous projects bound to send you running for your crochet hook and yarn. Learn to crochet everything from scarves, to bags, to sweaters and toys with patterns from crochet experts including Mary Jane Hall and Drew Emborsky. Show off your newly acquired skills by crocheting a beautiful sampler afghan square-by-square as you watch segments from the show on the enclosed DVD, highlighting those new stitches.

paperback with DVD; 8.25" × 10.875"; 128 pages
ISBN-10: 1-4402-1388-7
ISBN-13: 978-1-4402-1388-5
SRN: Z7967

These and other fine Krause Publications and North Light Craft titles are available at your local craft retailer, bookstore or online supplier, or visit our Web site at www.mycraftivitystore.com.